Tygers of Wrath

This book is one thing,
   Christ's curse is another.
He that stealeth the one,
   May God send him the other!

Anonymous English poet,
fifteenth century

TYGERS OF WRATH
Poems of Hate, Anger, and Invective

COLLECTED & EDITED by X. J. KENNEDY

Wood Engravings by Michael McCurdy

THE UNIVERSITY OF GEORGIA PRESS
Athens

Set in 10 on 14 point Mergenthaler Palatino type
Design by Michael McCurdy
Printed in the United States of America

Library of Congress Cataloging in Publication Data

Main entry under title:
Tygers of wrath.
Includes bibliographical references and index.
1. Invective. 2. English poetry. 3. American poetry.
I. Kennedy, X. J. II. Title: Hate, anger, and invective.
PR1195.I58T9   821'.008'0353   80-23212
ISBN 0-8203-0535-9

The tygers of wrath are wiser
than the horses of instruction.

William Blake
Proverbs of Hell

CONTENTS

III. SEXUAL SKIRMISHES

IV. Personal Animosities

VI. Nobles, Statesmen, Prelates, and Top Brass

VII. Poets, Critics, and Scholars

VIII. Offending Race of Humankind

IX. Damned Abstractions

X. This Vile Created World

XI. Self-loathing

ACKNOWLEDGMENTS

For permission to include copyrighted material, the following acknowledgments are gratefully made.

Alice James Books for "Warming Up for the Real Thing" from *Curses & Songs & Poems* by Lee Rudolph, Alice James Books, 1974, published by Alice James Poetry Cooperative, Inc., 138 Mount Auburn St., Cambridge, Mass. 02138.
George Allen & Unwin Ltd. for "The Curse" from *Poems and Translations* by John Millington Synge, 1950.
Alta for "I Don't Have No Bunny Tail on My Behind" from *Poems and Prose* by Alta. Copyright © 1969 by Alta.
Jack Anderson for "The Invention of New Jersey" from *The Invention of New Jersey* by Jack Anderson, University of Pittsburgh Press, 1969.
Atheneum Publishers, Inc., for "The Cost of Pretending" from "Pretending to Be Asleep" in *Walking the Boundaries* by Peter Davison. Copyright © 1967, 1968, 1969, 1970, 1974 by Peter Davison. For "An Old Malediction" from *The Venetian Vespers* by Anthony Hecht. Copyright © 1979 by Anthony E. Hecht. For "No Foundation" by John Hollander from *Jiggery-Pokery* edited by Anthony Hecht and John Hollander. Copyright © 1966 by Anthony Hecht and John Hollander. For "The Lady's-Maid's Song" from *Spectral Emanations: New and Selected Poems* by John Hollander. Copyright © 1958 by Yale University Press; copyright © 1979 by John Hollander. Used by permission of Atheneum Publishers.
Eloise S. Bender for "The Californians" by Theodore Spencer. Copyright © 1944, 1972 by The New Yorker Magazine, Inc.
BOA Editions for "Dr. Joseph Goebbels—22 April, 1945" by W. D. Snodgrass from *The Führer Bunker: A Cycle of Poems in Progress* by W. D. Snodgrass. Copyright © 1977 by W. D. Snodgrass. For "A Curse Against the Owner" by Barton Sutter from *Cedarhome* by Barton Sutter, foreword by W. D. Snodgrass. Copyright © 1977 by Barton Sutter. Reprinted with the permission of BOA Editions.
Broadside Press for quotation from "The Self-Hatred of Don L. Lee" from *Black Pride* by Don L. Lee. Copyright © 1968 by Don L. Lee.
Burning Deck for "Introducing a Madman" from *The Garden of Effort* by Keith Waldrop, Burning Deck, 1975. Copyright © 1970, 1975 by Keith Waldrop.
James Camp for "The Figure in the Carpet" from *Carnal Refreshment* by James Camp, Burning Deck, 1975. Copyright © 1975 by James E. Camp.
Jonathan Cape Ltd. and the Estate of William Plomer for "The Playboy of the Demi-World, 1938" from *Collected Poems* by William Plomer, 1960.
Carcanet Press Ltd. for "Human Relations" from *In the Trojan Ditch* by C. H. Sisson, Carcanet Press, Manchester, U.K. Copyright © 1974 by C. H. Sisson.
City Lights Books for "Uptown" from *Reality Sandwiches* by Allen Ginsberg. Copyright © 1968 by Allen Ginsberg. Reprinted by permission of City Lights Books.
Joseph P. Clancy for quotation from "The Rattle Bag" by Dafydd ap Gwilym from *Medieval Welsh Lyrics* translated by Joseph P. Clancy, St. Martin's Press, 1965.
Clarke, Irwin & Co. Ltd. for "The Loneliness of the Long Distance Runner" from *Bread, Wine and Salt* by Alden Nowlan. Copyright © 1967 by Clarke, Irwin & Co. Ltd. Used by permission.
Wesli Court for "Academic Curse: An Epitaph" and his version of "The Blacksmiths" from *Curses and Laments* by Wesli Court (Stevens Point, Wis.: Song, 1978). Copyright © 1978 by Richard Behm, copyright reversion to the author on publication; copyright © 1980 by Wesli Court. All rights reserved.
Curtis Brown, Ltd. for "The Traveler's Curse after Misdirection" from *Welchman's Hose* by Robert Graves. Copyright © 1925 by Robert Graves. For "The Glutton" from *Collected Poems 1955* by Robert Graves. Copyright © 1955 by Robert Graves. Reprinted by permission of Curtis Brown, Ltd.
Joan Daves for "Love and Hate" and "Inheritance" from *Kings, Lords, & Commons: An Anthology from the Irish* translated by Frank O'Connor. Copyright © 1959 by the Estate of Frank O'Connor.
The Devin-Adair Co. for "The Road to Hate" from *Collected Poems* by Patrick Kavanagh. Reprinted by permission of the Devin-Adair Co., Old Greenwich, Conn. 06870. Copyright © 1964 by Patrick Kavanagh.
The Dial Press for "The Complete Misanthropist" from *A Bowl of Bishop* by Morris Bishop. Copyright © 1954 by Morris Bishop. Reprinted by permission of the Dial Press.
Emanuel diPasquale for his poem "Incantation to Get Rid of a Sometime Friend."
Doubleday & Co., Inc. for passages from "The Four Zoas" which appeared in *The Poetry and Prose of William Blake*, edited by David V. Erdman. Copyright © 1965 by David V. Erdman and Harold Bloom. Reprinted by permission of Doubleday & Co., Inc. For "The Gods of the Copybook Headings," copyright 1919 by Rudyard Kipling, and lines from "The Beginnings," copyright 1917 by Rudyard Kipling, from *Rudyard Kipling's Verse: Definitive Edition*. Reprinted by permission of the Executors of the Estate of Mrs. George Bambridge and Doubleday & Co., Inc. For

Dennis Wepman, Ronald B. Newman, and Murray B. Binderman; Philadelphia: University of Pennsylvania Press, 1976.

The University of Pittsburgh Press for "Blank Verse for a Fat Demanding Wife" from *In Lieu of Mecca* by Jim Lindsey. Copyright © 1976 by Jim Lindsey. For "For a Friend" from *Body Compass* by David Steingass. Copyright © 1969 by the University of Pittsburgh Press. Both selections by permission of the University of Pittsburgh Press.

The University of Utah Press for "Campaign Promise" from *An Afternoon of Pocket Billiards* by Henry Taylor (Salt Lake City: University of Utah Press, 1975), page 25. Copyright © 1975 by Henry Taylor.

Wake Forest University Press for "The Pill" from *Selected Poems* by Austin Clarke, edited by Thomas Kinsella. Copyright © 1976 by Nora Clarke.

Wesleyan University Press for "One Poet Visits Another" from *The Complete Poems of W. H. Davies*. Copyright © 1963 by Jonathan Cape Ltd. For "The Business Life" from *Figures of the Human* by David Ignatow. Copyright © 1955 by David Ignatow. For "Animals Are Passing from Our Lives" from *Not This Pig* by Philip Levine. Copyright © 1968 by Philip Levine. For "In Response to a Rumor That the Oldest Whorehouse in Wheeling, West Virginia, Has Been Condemned" from *Collected Poems* by James Wright. Copyright © 1966 by James Wright. All selections reprinted by permission of Wesleyan University Press.

Dallas Wiebe for his poem "Epilogue" from *In the Late, Gnat Light* (The Art Association of Cincinnati, Inc., 1965).

Viking Penguin, Inc., for "Shitty" from *Collected Poems 1944–1979* by Kingsley Amis. Copyright © 1979 by Kingsley Amis. For "Meditation on a Bone" from *Collected Poems* by A. D. Hope. Copyright © 1960, 1966 by A. D. Hope. For "Gas from a Burner" from *Collected Poems* by James Joyce. Copyright © 1946, 1947, © renewed 1974, 1975 by The Viking Press, Inc. For "How Beastly the Bourgeois Is—" and "Willy Wet-Leg" from *The Complete Poems of D. H. Lawrence* edited by Vivian de Sola Pinto and F. Warren Roberts. Copyright © 1964, 1971 by Angelo Ravagli and C. M. Weekley, Executors of the Estate of Frieda Lawrence Ravagli. For "The General" from *Collected Poems* by Siegfried Sassoon. Copyright 1918 by E. P. Dutton & Co.; copyright renewed 1946 by Siegfried Sassoon. All selections reprinted by permission of Viking Penguin, Inc.

Georges-Denis Zimmermann for the text of "Skin the Goat's Curse on Carey" from *Songs of Irish Rebellion* edited by Georges-Denis Zimmermann (Folklore Associates, 1967).

INTRODUCTION

I

"The doctrine of hatred," said Emerson, "must be preached as the counteraction of the doctrine of love, when that pules and whines." So many anthologies have been devoted to the poetry of love that it seemed high time for the poetry of hate to have one. It was an especially puling and whining anthology called *Heart Throbs* that led me to this conviction, and a luminous suggestion by the critic John Press. Noting that the two dominant British poetry anthologies of the past century, Palgrave's *Golden Treasury* and Quiller-Couch's *Oxford Book of English Verse*, seem "disfigured" by a conception of the poet as lofty-minded, Press finds them lacking in works that express hatred, obscenity, lust, ferocity, and bitterness. Scarcely a poem hints that "man eats, drinks, commits fornication, dances, plays games, makes jokes, gossips, and runs away in the hour of battle."[1] Humankind appears in their pages as an ethereal spirit, diverted only by rainbows and primroses, smiling in beatific glee when splashed by a passing omnibus.

I have ventured to act upon only a small part of Press's immense suggestion, and to gather a various sampling of the poetry of hate, paying secondary notice to anger. From much poetry of hate, anger seems inseparable. Not all these poems are *expressions* of hatred. Some discern the workings of hatred in others, or take the nature of hate for theme. In order to complete my task before I die, I have represented only poets who write in English. Like poetry itself, however, the poetry of hate would seem worldwide. From the Old Testament, any universal anthology surely would contain many sublime descriptions of God's wrath, such as the inventory of the wicked man's heritage in Job 20:4–29; Psalm 137, with its address to the daughter of Babylon, "Happy shall he be, that taketh and dasheth thy little ones against the stones"; the preaching of Ecclesiastes that not only love but also hate has its season; and the several pieces of bitter invective in Ezekiel and Jeremiah. Classical literature would yield gems from Catullus, Horace, and Sextus Propertius; from the plays of Sophocles, whom hatred appears to have fascinated: the fatherly curse of the blind Oedipus upon Polyneices in *Oedipus at Colonus*, the several curses and fierce complaints of the heroine of the *Electra*. Goliardic

---

1. *The Fire and the Fountain*, second edition (London: Methuen, 1966), pp. 28–29.

verse of the Middle Ages would reward the winnower—for a single fine instance, see "Golias Curses a Thief" in the deft translation by George F. Whicher. The thief is wished, among other things, "agonies of excruciating purity."[2] Goethe and Rilke, Dante and Lorca and Calderón would testify, not to mention Pushkin, and Yevtushenko with his hatred of the haters of Jews in "Babi Yar."

Among certain primitive peoples, the recitation of a hateful chant or song is undoubtedly a powerful component of magic, a mutilation or destruction of a victim by means of words, much as a sorcerer works black magic by ritually injuring or burning a likeness of the victim, or an object representing him.[3] In Jerome Rothenberg's rich anthology of primitive songs and chants, the reader is struck by the frequency of curses and vituperations. Before going into battle, a Cherokee warrior casts a verbal spell against his enemy; while in Africa, a Hausa marksman utters a venomous incantation over his poisoned arrow before letting it fly. The surly Dobu of New Guinea rise to flights of poetry in a malicious charm ("To Cause the Gansoa That Eats Away the Nose"), and in Polynesia, a Magaian chieftain whose son has drowned sings his protest against the god who allowed the catastrophe: "Let piss and shit dribble down your fat cheeks, you bum god. Any man can do better."[4]

How should not poetry in English abound in wrath and loathing? The curious notion that the English people have been slow and reluctant haters is set forth in Kipling's poem "The Beginnings (1914–18)":

> *It was not part of their blood,*
> *It came to them very late*
> *With long arrears to make good,*
> *When the English began to hate.*

But much of the passion that flowered into *The Vision of Piers Plowman* is righteous rage: Langland's shocked dismay that peasants are treated so. A more joyous hatred informs the vigorous fifteenth-century lines against blacksmiths, "Swarte-smeked smethes . . ." The

---

2. *The Goliard Poets* (New York: New Directions, 1949), p. 287.

3. See Bronislaw Malinowski, *Magic, Science, and Religion* (New York: Doubleday, 1954), p. 71.

4. *Technicians of the Sacred: A Range of Poetries from Africa, America, Asia, and Oceania* (New York: Doubleday, 1968), pp. 70–74, 343.

Child ballads, for all their glamorizations of the nobility, are unsparing in their portraits of people in hatred's thrall—most wonderfully in the ballad of "Edward." Low comedy, popular ballads of domestic friction such as the "Wife Wrapt in Wether's Skin" (Child 277) are still memorable. In "The Farmer's Curst Wife" (Child 278), a shrewish spouse is foisted off on Satan, who refuses to keep her:

> *She spied thirteen imps all dancing in chains,*
> *She ups with her pattens and beats out their brains.*

Nursery rhymes, which Apollinaire called the oldest fossils of living poetry, abound in childish spell-casting, as in this Mother Goose jingle for taunting a tattletale:

> *Spit, cat, spit!*
> *Your tongue shall be slit!*
> *All the dogs in our town*
> *Shall have a little bit!*

Surely one of the longest traditions in English verse is that of outrageous political satire, spilling over into hate—as witness the lineage descending from Andrew Marvell to the topical poets of weekly news-reviews. Perhaps it is proof that the tradition still flourishes to note that, when the *New Statesman* held a weekly competition for the best poem beginning, "How do I hate thee? Let me count the ways," the overwhelmingly favorite subject was the prime minister.[5]

II

If such curses are among the piquant fruits of English poetry, in Celtic poetry the curse is a weighty branch, and the very tree seems rooted in invective. In "The Rebel Scot," John Cleveland paints a self-portrait of the poet consumed with wrath, harking back to the figure of the feared master poet of Celtic tradition:

> *Ring the bells backward; I am all on fire!*
> *Not all the buckets in a country choir*
> *Shall quench my rage. A poet should be feared*
> *When angry, like a comet's flaming beard.*

5. *New Statesman,* 14 July 1972.

But the English poet wears an evident smirk. He does not expect men to fear him, as they truly feared many a Scottish poet and prophet—notably Thomas of Erceldoune—and many a Welsh bard or Irish *ollave*. As Robert Graves has observed, "Let a man offer the least indignity to an Irish poet, even centuries after he had forfeited his priestly function to the Christian cleric, and he would compose a satire on his assailant which would bring out black blotches on his face and turn his bowels to water, or throw a 'madman's wisp' in his face and drive him insane."[1] Welsh minstrels wrote curses distinguished by power and complexity, while the great courtly poet Dafydd ap Gwilym had an invective at his command that has not lost force since the fourteenth century, even when filtered through translation. In "The Rattle Bag," the poet tells of his lying down with a woman outdoors in the summer, only to have her frightened away by "an imp in shepherd's shape" playing a rattle bag, a kind of drum filled with stones, used to scare off wild animals.

> By Christ, no Christian country,
> Cold harsh tune, has heard the like.
> Noisy pouch perched on a pole,
> Bell of pebbles and gravel,
> Saxon rocks making music
> Quaking in a bullock's skin,
> Crib of three thousand beetles,
> Commotion's cauldron, black bag,
> Field-keeper, comrade of straw,
> Black-skinned, pregnant with splinters,
> Noise that's an old buck's loathing,
> Devil's bell, stake in its crotch,
> Scarred pebble-bearing belly,
> May it be sliced into thongs.
> May the churl be struck frigid,
> Amen, who scared off my girl.[2]

Some of this tradition is still perceptible in a quieter curse by the eighteenth-century Welsh poet Evan Thomas, "To the Noble Woman of Llanarth Hall, who shut the author's goat in a house for two days, its crime being that it grazed too near the Mansion":

1. *The White Goddess* (New York: Vintage Books, 1958), p. 9.
2. Translation by Joseph P. Clancy, *Medieval Welsh Lyrics* (New York: St. Martins, 1965), pp. 34–35.

O black-maned, horse-haired, unworthy one,
What did you do to the goat, your sister?
She'd your father's horns, your mother's beard—
Why did you put her falsely in prison?[3]

In Scottish poetry, hate was at high tide at the end of the Middle Ages in the celebrated flytings, or battles of insult, rendered into poetry by William Dunbar for the amusement of the court of Scotland's James IV. The 152-line "Flyting of Dunbar and Kennedy" ends with a stupendous verbal crushing of its opponent:

Mauch muttoun, byt buttoun, peilit gluttoun, air to Hilhous;
Rank beggar, ostir dregar, foule fleggar in the flet;
Chittirlilling, ruch rilling, lik schilling in the milhous;
Baird rehator, theif of natur, fals tratour, feyindis gett;
Filling of tauch, rak sauch, cry crauch, thow art oursett;
Muttoun dryver, girnall ryver, yadswyvar, fowll fell the;
Herretyk, lunatyk, purspyk, carlingis pet,
Rottin crok, dirtin dok, cry cok, or I sall quell the.[4]

For a flyting somewhat closer in language to modern English, by an Englishman, I have included Skelton's defense of his honor as a poet against Garnesche.[5] Battles of insult may be at least as old and far-flung as civilization.[6] In our own century, blacks in American inner cities have enjoyed the game called the "Dozens," rhyming insult-

3. Translation by Anthony Conran, *The Penguin Book of Welsh Verse* (Harmondsworth, Middlesex, and Baltimore: Penguin, 1967), p. 208.

4. Readers for whom the language offers no hardship may wish to consult the full text in Dunbar's *Poems*, edited by James Kinsley (Oxford University Press, 1958). Some will assert that the whole of Dunbar's dirty calumny on the name of Kennedy should have gone into this book, but not I.

5. For an excellent discussion of Scottish flytings, see G. Legman. Giving choice samples from the 32-page alliterative "Flyting betwixt Polwart and Montgomery" (ca. 1580), Legman draws connections between this Scottish genre and the "Dozens" of urban black America. The name of the modern insult-contest comes from an Anglo-Scottish verb, *dozen*, to stun or stupify, still current in the term "bull-dozer." (*No Laughing Matter: Rationale of the Dirty Joke, Second Series*, New York: Breaking Point, 1975, pp. 782–97.)

6. J. Huizinga in *Homo Ludens* (Boston: Beacon Press, 1955), pp. 65–71, and Robert C. Elliott in *The Power of Satire* (Princeton: Princeton University Press, 1960), pp. 3–48, 70–84, offer fascinating discussions of insult-contests in Arabic, Greek, Levantine, Irish, Germanic and other languages. Robert Graves also cites instances of such contests in China and India, in his essay "'Lars Porsena,' or the Future of Swearing and Improper Language," *Occupation: Writer* (New York: Farrar, Straus and Cudahy, 1950).

jousts, in which the taunts are heaped higher and higher until one contestant loses his temper, or cannot reply.[7]

Not only in its resentments but in its poetry, Ireland for centuries has been a land of consummate ire. "No people hate as we do in whom that past is always alive," Yeats wrote in old age; "there are moments when hatred poisons my life and I accuse myself of effeminacy because I have not given it adequate expression."[8] Throughout his career, Yeats seems to have wavered between regarding hatred as a motivating force for poetry and as an ailment to be suffered. He had been torn, early in the century, between detesting Ireland's external foes and detesting his own countrymen, that seemingly dull and uneducable mass whom he damns as fumblers in a greasy till ("September 1913") and as eunuchs in Hell ("On Those That Hated 'The Playboy of the Western World,' 1907"). In "Easter 1916" he had come to the view that long fanatic anger petrifies the heart, yet in 1931, in "Remorse for Intemperate Speech," he was to regard the fanatic heart as the Irishman's inevitable heritage. In the phrase "great hatred, little room," Yeats sums up the situation of his country. Near the end of his days, in the great meditation "Ribh Considers Christian Love Insufficient," he was to turn again toward hatred as a cleansing and purifying fire, a necessary contrary to love in a universe of balanced dualities.

In early manhood, Yeats had assumed his legacy, a smoldering rage passed down like a cloak belonging to former poets. The tormented Mangan had worn it in praising "Dark Rosaleen," in the time of the great famine, and again in his version (based on scholarly cribs) of "O'Hussey's Ode to the Maguire." It was this lyric, by the last living master poet of the Maguire sect, whose *avran* or final summarizing stanza James Joyce thought superior in its way to all other passages of poetry in English, there being no rival in which "the spirit of revenge has been joined to such heights of melody":[9]

---

7. See John Dollard, "The Dozens: Dialect of Insult," *American Imago* 1 (1939): 3–25; and Roger D. Abrahams, "Playing the Dozens," *Journal of American Folklore* 75 (1962): 209–20.

8. "A General Introduction for My Work," written in 1937; *Essays and Introductions* (New York: Macmillan, 1961), p. 519.

9. *Critical Writings* (New York: Viking, 1959), p. 184. I am indebted for this citation to Malcolm Brown's indispensable study, *The Politics of Irish Literature: From Thomas Davis to W. B. Yeats* (Seattle: University of Washington Press, 1972), p. 91.

Hugh marched forth to the fight—I grieved to see him so depart;
And lo! tonight he wanders frozen, rain-drenched, sad, betrayed—
  But the memory of the lime-white mansions his right hand
    has laid
  In ashes warms the hero's heart!

The poetry of Irish hate would make a thick book in itself, and, if it admitted translations, would need to take in the "Song of Hate" by the early medieval Cadoc, who curses things in threes ("I hate journeys without safety, families without strength, and lawsuits without reason"). It would include the "Vision" of the twelfth-century Mac-Conglinne (a violent satire on the clergy); and the great twelfth or thirteenth-century narrative of Mad Sweeney, king of Dal Araidhe, who, according to the anonymous poet, confronted Saint Roan while in a rage, only to be cursed and dispatched to "wander forever and fly stark naked across the world." It would encompass the last masterpiece of Gaelic poetry, Brian Merriman's *The Midnight Court*;[10] and in English, the eighteenth-century Patrick O'Kelly's rhymed diatribe against the town in which someone stole his watch, "The Curse of Doneraile":

> *May ev'ry churn and milking pail*
> *Fall dry to staves in Doneraile.*
> *May cold and hunger still congeal*
> *The stagnant blood of Doneraile.*
> *May ev'ry hour new woes reveal*
> *That Hell reserves for Doneraile.*

There are eighty more lines of it. On his property's being replaced by Lady Doneraile herself, O'Kelly wrote a sequel, "Blessings on Doneraile," but this afterthought is greatly inferior, and has not had the same influence.[11] The poetry of Irish hate contains many elaborate

10. Arland Ussher's translation of Merriman's hilarious dream-vision appears, along with O'Kelly's "Curse" and excerpts from MacConglinne and the *Mad Sweeney*, in Kathleen Hoagland's *1000 Years of Irish Poetry* (New York: Devin-Adair, 1947). Other versions of *The Midnight Court* include that of David Marcus (Dublin: Dolmen, 1953; reprinted 1967) and that of Frank O'Connor in *Kings, Lords, and Commons* (New York: Alfred A. Knopf, 1959).

11. O'Kelly's inspiration shows, I believe, in the anonymous Australian "McQuade's Curse" ("May Satan, with a rusty crook, / Catch every goat in Tallarook"), included in

damnations of traitors and informers, notably J. J. Callanan's "Dirge of O'Sullivan Bear" ("May the hearth-stones of Hell / Be their best bed for ever!").[12] Such poems have Gaelic precedents. In his monumental *Religious Songs of Connacht* (1906), Douglas Hyde, the poet who became a president, translated from the Irish a number of comparable curses that he aptly called "evil prayer." From an anonymous nineteenth-century poet, Hyde took:

> *Bruadar and Smith and Glinn,*
> *Amen, dear God, I pray,*
> *May they lie low in waves of woe,*
> *And tortures slow each day!*
> *Amen!*

And so on for twenty-five more stanzas, each with its fixed final *Amen!*, calling down blindness, numb members, thirst without drink, the shaking ague, throat-decay, and, to be sure, the torments of Hell upon its miserable targets. It is a problem to write such a poem and avoid monotony, although the repetitiousness no doubt impresses the quaking victim. To pay some small homage to this tradition, I have included the anonymous "Skin the Goat's Curse upon Carey" and one unrepetitious curse translated by Frank O'Connor. (I have also had to break my rule against translations in order to put in O'Connor's great version of a poem about hatred itself.)

III

In recent America, protest poetry written against the war in Vietnam has yielded much that now seems merely dismal and dutiful, and several possibly lasting poison orchids. Few poets were to equal the bitterness of Robert Bly;[1] or that of Denise Levertov, who in "A

The Penguin Book of Australian Ballads (Harmondsworth, Middlesex, and Baltimore: Penguin, 1964) and other anthologies. It seems visible, too, in "Oh! Fucking Halkirk," an unfavorable comment on a town in the North of Scotland, sung by soldiers of the Ayrshire Yeomanry (*'Kiss Me Goodnight, Sergeant Major': The Songs and Ballads of World War II*, edited by Martin Page [London: Hart-Davis, MacGibbon, 1973], pp. 44–45).

12. This poem by Callanan (1795–1829) may be found in Padraic Colum's *Anthology of Irish Verse* (New York: Liveright, 1972) and in W. H. Auden's *Nineteenth-Century Minor Poets* (London: Faber and Faber, 1966).

1. See individual poems in his collection *The Light Around the Body* (New York: Harper and Row, 1967).

Poem at Christmas, 1972, during the Terror-Bombing of North Vietnam," imagines herself serving as a waitress at Richard M. Nixon's inaugural feast. Hurling a container of napalm into the president's face, she whiffs his burning body-oils. After this promising beginning, the poem sputters out with an apology for being driven to such an extreme. It is as though the poet knows that she asks of herself a hatred greater than human.[2]

There were also lukewarm well-meaning protests, and endless solemn professions of personal dismay. For a time, in the latter part of the war, many poets appeared to have become professional beraters of the administration, basking in the klieg lights of success. Here and there, a skeptical voice was heard: that of Anthony Hecht, who expressed his doubts in an epigram—

> *Here lies fierce Strephon, whose poetic rage*
> *Lashed out on Viet Nam from page and stage;*
> *Whereby from basements of Bohemia he*
> *Rose to the lofts of sweet celebrity;*
> *Being, by Fortune, (our Eternal Whore)*
> *One of the few to profit by that war;*
> *A fate he shared—it bears much thinking on—*
> *With certain persons at the Pentagon.*[3]

Not that all poets who felt deeply about the war, and acted on their consciences, were hypocrites. Howard Nemerov, who expressed doubts similar to Hecht's in "On Being Asked for a Peace Poem," himself wrote a viciously good protest, "On Getting Out of Vietnam."[4] The poetry of those unhappy years is still being winnowed, and, unlike poets of earlier world wars, uniformed young poets who served in Vietnam were slow to report. I include one such war poem that remains for me strong as protest and as poetry, by Gibbons Ruark.

Venting a different anger, feminist poetry on both sides of the Atlantic has owed much to the life and work of Sylvia Plath, whose suicide many interpreted as martyrdom. As Elizabeth Hardwick has noticed, Plath "always seems to be describing her self-destruction as

2. Denise Levertov, *The Freeing of the Dust* (New York: New Directions, 1975), pp. 37–38.

3. One of a series, "A Little Cemetery," *Counter/Measures* 1 (1972): 15.

4. *The Collected Poems of Howard Nemerov* (Chicago: University of Chicago Press, 1977), pp. 428–29, 421.

an exhilarating act of contempt," and she aims tirades at male recipients, apparently husband and father.[5] Recently, Karl Shapiro in a sweeping complaint against the state of American poetry, has had dark thoughts about feminist poets who carve up all mankind. "The modality of most of the separatist cultural movements is hatred," Shapiro reproves, meaning black and feminist revolutionaries; and he cites with dismay a poem by a woman who imagines the lynching of Sylvia Plath's husband, Ted Hughes, by furious militants.[6] But what is wrong with such angry poems is not, I think, simply that they voice hate. Deeper problems arise from that contract of sympathy which, according to John Ciardi, poet and reader are always obliged to negotiate. Should the reader be repelled by the idea of lynching Ted Hughes, then the sympathetic contract is broken. It will probably be returned without signature.

For white readers, special contractual difficulties arise in much of the revolutionary black American poetry written since the mid-sixties. Unlike earlier black poems of mournful protest, recent work by Amiri Baraka, Don L. Lee, Nikki Giovanni, Bobb Hamilton, Larry Neal, and others explodes with cries of hatred and images of violence. "We want 'poems that kill,'" declares Baraka in his manifesto poem "Black Art." Figuratively, poems must crack steel knuckles into Jewish mouths, tear out policemen's tongues and send them back to Ireland. Similar treatment is prescribed for blacks who tolerate the white establishment.

How real is the hatred expressed in such poems? Some critics have wondered, with Arthur P. Davis, how much of their vitriol is conventional.[7] Yet there seems no reason to question the passionate convictions of Baraka, who more recently has gravitated toward a more traditional Leninist position; nor to doubt that, as Langston Hughes foresaw, a dream deferred may eventually explode. Less militant blacks, as well as whites, have been alienated from the new poetry of hate by its ferocious language and its imagery of excrement. Terence Collins, though, has defended this offensiveness. Blacks, he reasons, are going through a new crisis of identity. Having in the past felt shat upon, they now turn to heap verbal shit on their beshitters.[8]

---

5. *Seduction and Betrayal: Women and Literature* (New York: Random House, 1974), p.

6. Shapiro, "Creative Glut," *Poetry* 135 (October 1979): 36–49.

7. "The New Poetry of Black Hate," *CLA Journal* 33 (June 1970): 382–91.

8. "Self-Image through Imagery: Black Arts Poets and the Politics of Excrement," *Maledicta, the International Journal of Verbal Aggression* 3 (Summer 1979): 71–84.

Collins may well be right in arguing that black invective leveled at whites is meant not for white ears, but for home consumption. Certainly the new black poetry of hate has borne remarkable poems, if readers will sift to find them. For some revolutionary poets, though, mental hatred at times has stifled poetry. Michael S. Harper has perceived the danger inherent in tasting "a pickle of hate / so sour my mouth twicked / up and would not sing."[9]

IV

I have not the ambition to offer an aesthetic for hatred in poetry, nor the competence to speak from a grounding in psychology. But merely from having tried to understand why certain poems of hatred incandescently blaze, while others just sputter and fume, I would offer a few suspicions.

A satisfactory poem of hate cannot propose torments for its victim so extreme that the hater himself becomes ludicrous. Whitman's rejected poem "Respondez" fails to move us with its cry, "Let him who is without my poems be assassinated!" (Poets, no doubt, often have this wish, but only damned idiots among them utter it.) It is quite a different thing, of course, if the poem is deliberately comic. In order for the sympathetic contract to be sealed, the poet has to express a reasonable detestation with which the reader can side. Reading now, by the light of the Holocaust, the early T. S. Eliot's sneers at Klipstein, Bleistein, and Sir Ferdinand Klein, we are likely to feel ourselves embarrassed invitees to a ceremony we sense to be mean, however well-appointed its surroundings: a farting match in a Rolls Royce Silver Shadow.

Merely passive spite seldom generates poetic energy. Reading a poem of wholehearted hate, we can imagine the poet rushing headlong—as Whitman sees himself in his triumphant "Song of Myself"—"Hot toward the one I hate, ready in my madness to knife him." That will stand for a fair description of the tone of a good poem of hate, though the hatred be as coldly intense as in Pope's portrait of Sporus—a poem that, instead of rushing headlong, stands back with its long slim foil and flicks off its victim's buttons. It is not enough that

9. "Reuben, Reuben," in *Images of Kin: New and Selected Poems* (Urbana: University of Illinois Press, 1977), p. 198. The poem is not about interracial hatred, but about the death of a child in a hospital.

hatred be powerful and deeply felt; in addition, the emotional charge of the poem has to stay within its poet's control. An exception must be made again if humor is its object. Reading L. A. MacKay's "I Wish My Tongue Were a Quiver," we take pleasure in seeing the hater take off and whiz around, showering sparks like some demented catherine wheel.

Impelled by the power of hate, even pedestrian prose will sometimes soar into poetry. There is, for instance, an astonishing death sentence handed down by a U.S. District Court in 1881, taunting a convicted murderer with predictions of a spring he will not live to see:

> *From every tree top some wild woods songster will carol his mating song, butterflies will sport in the sunshine, the busy bee will hum happy as it pursues its accustomed vocation. The gentle breeze will tease the tassels of the wild grasses, and all nature, José Manuel Miguel Xavier Gonzales, will be glad but you. You won't be here to enjoy it because I command the sheriff or some other officer of this country to lead you out to some remote spot, swing you by the neck from a knotting bough of a sturdy oak, and let you hang until you are dead.*
>
> *And then, José Manuel Miguel Xavier Gonzales, I further command that such officer or officers retire quickly from your dangling corpse, that vultures may descend from the heavens upon your filthy body until nothing shall remain but bare, bleached bones of a cold-blooded, copper-colored, bloodthirsty, throat-cutting, chili-eating, sheep-herding, murdering son-of-a-bitch.*[1]

That is a bad poem, because it is unintentionally comic. The judge reveals himself not only as a blatant noose-swinger against whom no Mexican has a chance, but also as a frustrated nature poet in trite phrases such as *busy bee* and *gentle breeze*. What impresses is the way his diction improves as his hatred intensifies. A more famous instance of prose wafted aloft by rage is the letter to Emerson written by Swinburne in 1874, on reading a report that the sage of Concord had called him "a perfect leper, and a mere sodomite":

---

1. Found by Cleopatra Mathis in a verbatim transcript, *United States of America* v. *Gonzales*, 1881, in the records of the U.S. District Court, New Mexico Territory Sessions. For the whole of the transcript, see *Antaeus*, Autumn 1976.

A foul mouth is so ill-matched with a white beard that I would gladly believe the newspaper scribes alone responsible for the bestial utterances which they declare to be dropped from a teacher whom such disciples as these exhibit to our disgust and compassion as performing on their obscene platform the last tricks of tongue now possible to a gap-toothed and hoary-headed ape, carried at first into notice on the shoulder of Carlyle, and who now in his dotage spits and chatters from a dirtier perch of his own finding and fouling; coryphaeus or choragus of his Bulgarian tribe of autocoprophagous baboons, who make the filth they feed on.[2]

Pure joy in language is evident here, as in the "Dozens." In some poems, especially Irish ones, I find it difficult to be sure whether the poet's object is to destroy an enemy, or to revel in hatred's aphrodisiac boost to the vocabulary. There is ever the risk—at times, the promise—of a vilification's turning into such a tour de force that it somersaults over into merriment. Gorgeous verbiage studded with metaphor can be grand; and yet there is also a place for a kind of invective delivered with quiet authority. In his preface to "Fire, Famine, and Slaughter," Coleridge admires a certain sailor who could swear with "that sort of calmness of tone which is to the ear what the paleness of anger is to the eye." It is the tone, say, of Pope's best satiric devastations. In our day, when any word may appear in print and all words have dwindled in shock value, the poet of powerful calm may be the one best able to curse with efficacy.

Another means of control seems often an advantage: some kind of strict form, whether traditional or not. In the Irish curse against Bruadar, Smith, and Glinn, a metrical stanza and a refrain fix limits, help shape a ritual, and so keep the poet from ineffectually blathering. In certain folk poems, the device of rhyme appears to help in obtaining a bit of distance from a subject, and so permits the poet to curse with an impunity he might not otherwise feel. Legman has found an apparent need for rhyme in both the "Dozens" and in children's taunting jingles, citing an incisive passage from Martha Wolfenstein's study *Children's Humor*:

2. Reprinted in full by Joseph Rosner in *The Hater's Handbook*, a survey of abuse hurled at the famous (New York: Delacorte, 1965), pp. 142–43; and by Donald Carroll in *Dear Sir, Drop Dead!: Hate Mail through the Ages* (New York: Collier Books, 1979), p. 30.

What is the function of rhyme in these joking attacks? I would suggest that the first rhyming word has the effect of compelling the utterance of the second, thus reducing the speaker's responsibility. . . . There is a further reduction of responsibility in the use of a rhymed formula: the words are not my own. Moreover the rhyme is apt to induce other children to take it up; the attacker will cease to be alone.[3]

As Yeats knew, an intellectual hatred is the worst. In poetry, a hate-object cannot remain a cerebral abstraction for which the poet feels a merely opinionated detestation. If the poet selects an abstraction to hate, he had best do so for personal reasons. In "The Lamentation of the Old Pensioner," a poem Yeats revised over a span of fifty years, an old man curses Time. Working his lines into their final version, Yeats renders Time immediate and definite. It becomes the old man's intimate foe, it is given a face. Allen Ginsberg in "Howl" delivers himself of a final blast against the abstraction Moloch, on which he blames the evils in America. But I am better persuaded by Ginsberg's small poem "Uptown," with its realistic portrait of an all-American hippie-hater.

At least one virtue in Ginsberg's diatribe against Moloch, however, is that its object is appropriate to the poet's rhetoric. Good hate seems too valuable to waste on trivial offenders. Once more, humorous poems are exceptions. In James Stephens's "A Glass of Beer" or in the ballad "Nell Flaherty's Drake," comedy results from an incongruity between a powerful curse and its small occasion.

Prolonged hatred of things so enormous they can hardly be dented—such as the cosmos—is likely to rankle, turn against the hater, and eventually strike him mute. That is why hatred in poetry needs to be sharply focused, precisely aimed. Otherwise it is as risky to the poet as a stick of dynamite in the hand of a cross-eyed demolitionist. Hatred has to be got rid of. It ought to go off with a deafening boom, flinging spectators to the ground and giving its hurler the satisfaction of having leveled something. Recent literary magazines will yield countless sad poems whose hatred never is focused. All the reader can tell is that the poet, for reasons he never confides, would willingly blow up reader, himself, and the whole stinking universe,

3. Legman, *No Laughing Matter*, p. 788.

provided he could receive a grant to do it from the National Endowment for the Arts.

Such confused poems, I believe, have only given hatred a tawdry name in many quarters. An astute critic, Donald Davie, in an essay, "Art and Anger," has even declared hatred "essentially inartistic." Davie denies the assumption (on the part of someone setting a topic for an academic conference) that "the poet has a stake in . . . the forces which both create poetry and destroy social order," and he pays tribute to Pope as a great angry attacker of order-destroyers. Unsuccessful recent poems of protest show Davie right on that point, for most calls to senseless violence tend to emerge in senseless language that sprawls on its rump with its pants down, making animal noises. But it grieves me that Davie has nothing favorable to say for hatred, which he categorizes with sterile impulses such as rancor and indignation. What he admires is that "cleanness and clarity of anger" to be found in the work of Yeats and Pope.[4]

There are times, I agree, when to distinguish between anger and hatred is both possible and helpful. Parents, to take a common example, often feel anger toward their children without hating them. And there is surely a difference in tone between the sonnet of Milton, his shock and sorrow mingled, damning the "bloody Piemontese" and the same poet's angry—also, I think, profoundly hating—lines on the corrupt clergy in "Lycidas." A problem, only for critics, is that distinctions between anger and hatred will not stay made. To be sure, there is a dull, sniveling, passive kind of hatred—the kind, I gather, that Davie despises—that produces no poetry, any more than does a wormish glow of quasi-hearted love. Yet, as John Wain remarked, "Hatred can be ink in a poet's pen." Invective can be an instrument for social reform, in the view of F. R. Scott and A. J. M. Smith, editors of an anthology of poems sharply critical of Canadian morals, manners, and politics.[5] Shared hatred can bind men into brotherhood, as recent black poets have known, and as Dryden knew when in his elegy for Oldham he recalled: "And knaves and fools we both abhorred alike."

One contemporary poet to whom hatred appears essential is J. V. Cunningham, the speaker of whose poem 'Dark thoughts are my

4. *Trying to Explain* (Ann Arbor: University of Michigan Press, 1979), pp. 52–56.

5. *The Blasted Pine: An Anthology of Satire, Invective and Disrespectful Verse Chiefly by Canadian Writers*, revised edition (Toronto: Macmillan, 1967).

companions' declares hatred his redemption, love his foe. Trying to make sense out of what he calls Cunningham's "doctrine of hatred, or anger," Yvor Winters has observed,

> *The doctrine, briefly, and as nearly as I can understand it, is that hatred is the only cleansing emotion and the most moral of emotions. Baldly put, the doctrine is not beguiling and may even seem shocking, but it is not without justification in experience.*[6]

V

The arrangement of this book is not haphazard, but rather than blabbing on about it (like that long-winded orator who continued his speech to the Dail, "And in the forty-third place—"), I will trust that patient readers will see it for themselves. But I owe some apologies to those who will feel that too many great poems are left out. The tradition of English satire has given this book some of its higher moments, but as a general thing I have chosen only satiric works that rage, eke venom, or sweep away the satirist from his perch of lofty superiority. It would seem more natural for a poet to hate those who have power over him, or to hate his peers, than to hate his mere helpless inferiors. But a larger anthology than this one would have included the whole *Dunciad*, all of "Absalom and Achitophel" and "The Vision of Judgment," and a good deal of *Don Juan*, by poets whose great works I have tried to remember in self-contained excerpts. But these are best read entire, and they are readily available. Verse narratives of crime, I soon found, are not necessarily hateful or angry. In broadside ballads, the poet's attitude toward the most dastardly violence is often sympathetic, curious, and affectionate, for all his pious platitudes. Ample collections of the poetry of crime will be found elsewhere.[1] I haven't tried to do justice to the poetry of stomach-turning horror or repugnance, many samples of which appear in George Macbeth's remarkable *Penguin Book of Sick Verse*. Women, children, and family are

6. "The Poetry of J. V. Cunningham," Swallow Pamphlets no. 11 (Denver: Swallow, 1961), p. 8.

1. For a start, see *Bloody Versicles* by Jonathan Goodman (Newton Abbot, Devon: 1971) and *American Murder Ballads* by Olive Woolley Burt (New York: Oxford University Press, 1958; paperbound reprint, Citadel, 1964).

the objects of hateful ridicule in much comic, bawdy verse; but most of it seems mean, snickering stuff, afraid to bring its hatred out in the open. Alone among major poets, Wordsworth seems to have had little fancy for hate. Here and there in *The Prelude* he has a kind word for hatred of social injustice, but his well-known sonnet beginning "Degenerate Douglas! oh, the unworthy Lord!" delivers a mere twittery rap across that tree-destroying nobleman's knuckles. I came across very little blasphemy that seemed passable poetry, other than Gary Snyder's "Xrist," and offer no section of it. Unless one is Milton's Satan, it seems hard to be against the Hebrew-Christian God on general principle.

Evidently, hatred is heavy going, and I trust the reader will welcome an occasional bit of light verse or popular poetry for relief. I confess to an early fondness for such spiteful fluff, ever since hearing my father recite a rhyme remembered from his own childhood. Current about 1895 in Wharton, New Jersey, it was a taunt that boys hurled at passing vessels from the banks of the Morris Canal:

Oh, you dirty canaler, you'll never get rich!
You'll die in the cabin like a dog in a ditch!

("Many a canalboatman we'd holler that at, and they'd come out of the cabin, if we were lucky, and throw bottles at us.") In *my* childhood, verse of a low order thrived in garishly illustrated comic valentines sold for two cents in a local dimestore, as in this one, to be sent to a laborer:

You lazy shirk with ape-like mug!
Honest work you hate, but love the jug.
Booze is taking you to the grave with speed
Where you'll poison the worms that on you feed.[2]

Despite the flaws in their syntax, such pulp-paper broadside items generated a magnetic energy. Their crude jingles stuck in my head more firmly than innocuous poems that my old gray teachers were championing. Perhaps I had dimly glimpsed what Blake meant in picking the tygers of wrath over the horses of instruction.

No careful reader, I trust, will think me blind to the evils of hatred and wrath when expressed in deeds by men of ruthless will.

2. Bought in Grant's, Dover, New Jersey, about 1937.

None of us dares to forget the Nazi holocaust, or the destruction of Hiroshima, and I would not wish for greater hatred on earth than there is already. By gathering these poems, I mean simply to question a certain critical sentimentality, the attitude of those who would ignore or deny the pervasive force of hatred in English-speaking poetry. I admit to a further hope. Should any poets leaf through this book and be encouraged to hone their own deep hatreds into successful poetry, I will be thankful. In a poem, "Robot Feelings," D. H. Lawrence condemns a certain "grinding, nihilistic hate," the one passion of which emotionally blunted modern man is still capable. Indeed, those readers who follow contemporary poetry will probably have had their fill of robot hate poems, that seem ground out, and of— even more prevalent—quite coolly disinterested poems, rattled out of electric typewriters. In our poetic climate, a small rain of truly heartfelt hate ought to be welcome. Wetted, refreshed, we might then admit the dismaying wholeness of our human natures. We might remember that in poetry, as Ezra Pound tells us, only emotion endures.

If anthologists had a right to dedications, this book would be dedicated (without malice) to William Cole. Over a decade while I worked on it, he continually sent me copies of poems for it, out of his own extensive store. Timothy Dickinson probed his wide knowledge of poetry for many more fine suggestions than I could follow. Others who aided with advice, permissions, or texts include L. Elizabeth Hardin of Gale Research, Sheldon Harnick, Stanley W. Lindberg, Bernard McCabe, John Frederick Nims, Gibbons Ruark, Knute Skinner, Lewis Turco, David Wagoner, Keith and Rosmarie Waldrop, and Peter Williams. Dorothy M. Kennedy patiently improved my manuscript. In his editorial capacity, Paul Zimmer discouraged me from including any of his own poems of hatred and anger, but those who will seek them out will love them well.

Farrar, Straus and Giroux, publishers, objected to what they deemed my classification of their poets as "haters." Had they not denied permission, I would have included the following poems: "Dream Song 365" from *The Dream Songs* by John Berryman (1969); "Several Voices out of a Cloud" from *The Blue Estuaries* by Louise Bogan (1968); "Posterity" from *High Windows* by Philip Larkin (1974); "The Banker's Daughter" from *Life Studies* by Robert Lowell (1959); "Intellectual Detachment" from *Collected Poems 1918–1976* by Allen Tate (1977); and "Party Night at the Hilton" from *Sea Grapes* by Derek Walcott (1976).

A NOTE ON THE TEXT

An asterisk following the title of a poem indicates that a note on that poem will be found at the back of the book. When the first line of a poem is its only title, that title is given within single quotation marks. Brackets indicate titles supplied by convention, or by the editor. Texts have been made regular and spellings modern unless to do so would alter meter or sound. Certain poems, however, are not altered in cases of eccentric usage that seems essential. Blake's songs, already familiar in conventional spelling and punctuation, have been kept that way; but Blake's curse on Urizen is given in the edition of David V. Erdman; and Emily Dickinson's 'Mine Enemy is growing old,' in the edition of Thomas H. Johnson.

I.

IN PRAISE
OF HATE

Arise, black vengeance, from thy hollow cell!
Yield up, O love, thy crown and hearted throne
To tyrannous hate!

WILLIAM SHAKESPEARE, *Othello*

I asked the red-hot iron, when it glimmered on the anvil,
"Wherefore glowest thou longer than the fire-brand?"
"I was born in the dark mine, and the brand in the pleasant
    greenwood."
Kindness fadeth away, but vengeance endureth.

SIR WALTER SCOTT, "Verses in the Style of the Druids"

Now hatred is by far the longest pleasure;
Men love in haste, but they detest at leisure.

GEORGE GORDON, LORD BYRON, *Don Juan*

Anyone who hates children and dogs can't be all bad.

W. C. FIELDS

FIRE AND ICE

Some say the world will end in fire,
Some say in ice.
From what I've tasted of desire
I hold with those who favor fire.
But if it had to perish twice,
I think I know enough of hate
To say that for destruction ice
Is also great
And would suffice.

Robert Frost

A POISON TREE

I was angry with my friend:
I told my wrath, my wrath did end.
I was angry with my foe:
I told it not, my wrath did grow.

And I watered it in fears,
Night and morning with my tears;
And I sunned it with smiles,
And with soft deceitful wiles.

And it grew both day and night,
Till it bore an apple bright;
And my foe beheld it shine,
And he knew that it was mine,

And into my garden stole

When the night had veiled the pole:
In the morning glad I see
My foe outstretched beneath the tree.

William Blake

/ LOVE AND HATE

Hate only will I love,
    Love I will set aside,
The misery of love
    Too many a heart has tried.

My scorn upon the thing
    That such vain grief began
And many a good man made
    Into a sick man.

Even when it goes too far
    Hate's the better part,
One can bid Hate pack,
    Who can bid love depart?

Hate is healthy fare
    That leaves the body sound,
Nor herb nor medicine cures
    Love's bitter wound.

Once I saw a girl
    Choose a man in play;
Love he never knew
    To his dying day.

I whate'er befall
    Know a better fate—
This is all my song,
    I will love only hate.

Frank O'Connor

RIBH CONSIDERS
CHRISTIAN LOVE INSUFFICIENT*

Why should I seek for love or study it?
It is of God and passes human wit.
I study hatred with great diligence,
For that's a passion in my own control,
A sort of besom that can clear the soul
Of everything that is not mind or sense.

Why do I hate man, woman or event?
That is a light my jealous soul has sent.
From terror and deception freed it can
Discover impurities, can show at last
How soul may walk when all such things are past,
How soul could walk before such things began.

Then my delivered soul herself shall learn
A darker knowledge and in hatred turn
From every thought of God mankind has had.
Thought is a garment and the soul's a bride
That cannot in that trash and tinsel hide:
Hatred of God may bring the soul to God.

At stroke of midnight soul cannot endure
A bodily or mental furniture.

What can she take until her Master give!
Where can she look until He make the show!
What can she know until He bid her know!
How can she live till in her blood He live!

William Butler Yeats

LINES FOR AN OLD MAN

The tiger in the tiger-pit
Is not more irritable than I.
The whipping tail is not more still
Than when I smell the enemy
Writhing in the essential blood
Or dangling from the friendly tree.
When I lay bare the tooth of wit
The hissing over the archèd tongue
Is more affectionate than hate,
More bitter than the love of youth,
And inaccessible by the young.
Reflected from my golden eye
The dullard knows that he is mad.
Tell me if I am not glad!

T. S. Eliot

THE SAVAGE BEAST

As I leaned to retrieve
my property
he leaped with all his weight
so that I felt

the wind of his jaws
as his teeth gnashed
before my mouth.
Isn't he awful! said

the woman, his collar
straining under her clutch.
Yes, I replied drily
wanting to eviscerate

the thing there, scoop
out his brains
and eat them—and hers
too! Until it flashed

on me, How many, like
this dog, could I not wish
had been here in my
place, only a little closer!

William Carlos Williams

ZEAL AND LOVE

Oxford. November 20, 1832.

And would'st thou reach, rash scholar mine,
   Love's high unruffled state?
Awake! thy easy dreams resign,
   First learn thee how to hate:—

Hatred of sin, and Zeal, and Fear,
   Lead up the Holy Hill:

Track them, till Charity appear
  A self-denial still.

Dim is the philosophic flame
  By thoughts severe unfed:
Book-lore ne'er served, when trial came,
  Nor gifts, when faith was dead.

John Henry Cardinal Newman

THE ROAD TO HATE

He said: The road you are going will lead you to Hate
For I went down that way yesterday and saw it away
In the hollow a mile distant and I turned back
Glad of my escape.
        But I said: I will persist,
For I know a man who went down the hill into the hollow
And entered the very city of Hate
And God visited him every day out of pity
Till in the end he became a most noble saint.

Patrick Kavanagh

'DARK THOUGHTS ARE MY COMPANIONS'

Dark thoughts are my companions. I have wined
With lewdness and with crudeness, and I find
Love is my enemy, dispassionate hate
Is my redemption though it come too late—
Though I come to it with a broken head
In the cat-house of the dishevelled dead.

J. V. Cunningham

I WOKE UP. REVENGE

I woke up. Revenge was in my mouth.
I said my prayers. It tasted good,
familiar, old. I didn't feel afraid.

I have survived ten years of stale
nicotine and gin, a decade of most
kinds of sin. But I can't brush it
off my teeth or gargle it out of my throat.

And on my tongue revenge still sits,
a recalcitrant wedge of thinnest bread,
a stubborn, undissolving vatican.

A. Poulin, Jr.

THE MEN'S ROOM IN THE COLLEGE CHAPEL

Here, in the most Unchristian basement
of this "fortress for the Christian mind,"
they close these four gray walls, shut out shame,
and scribble of sex and excrement,
draw bestial pictures and sign their name—
the old, lewd defiance of mankind.

The subversive human in his cell—
burn his vile books, stamp out his credo,
lock him away where no light falls,
and no live word can go back to tell
where he's entombed like Monte Cristo—
still, he'll carve his platform in the walls.

In need, men have painted the deep caves
to summon their animal, dark gods;
even the reviled, early Christians
prayed in catacombs to outlawed Good,
laid their honored dead and carved out graves
with pious mottos of resistance.

This is the last cave, where the soul
turns in its corner like a beast
nursing its wounds, where it contemplates
vengeance, how it shall gather to full
strength, what lost cause shall it vindicate,
returning, masterless and twisted.

W. D. Snodgrass

THE WHITE CITY*

I will not toy with it nor bend an inch.
Deep in the secret chambers of my heart
I muse my life-long hate, and without flinch
I bear it nobly as I live my part.
My being would be a skeleton, a shell,
If this dark Passion that fills my every mood,
And makes my heaven in the white world's hell,
Did not forever feed me vital blood.
I see the mighty city through a mist—
The strident trains that speed the goaded mass,
The poles and spires and towers vapor-kissed,
The fortressed port through which the great ships pass,
The tides, the wharves, the dens I contemplate,
Are sweet like wanton loves because I hate.

Claude McKay

/ 'INDEED INDEED, I CANNOT TELL'

Indeed indeed, I cannot tell,
Though I ponder on it well,
Which were easier to state,
All my love or all my hate.
Surely, surely, thou wilt trust me
When I say thou dost disgust me.
O, I hate thee with a hate
That would fain annihilate;
Yet sometimes against my will,
My dear friend, I love thee still.
It were treason to our love,
And a sin to God above,
One iota to abate
Of a pure impartial hate.

Henry David Thoreau

BETTER TO SPIT ON THE WHIP
THAN STUTTER YOUR LOVE LIKE A WORM

Better to spit
on the whip
that drives you
to dead work
where lashing clocks
will welt your back

than rot flint-hearted,
venomous and squat
like senators of war,
old men cloaked in wisdom
stuttering their love.

Colette Inez

MEDITATION ON A BONE

A piece of bone, found at Trondhjem in 1901, with the following runic
inscription (about A.D. 1050) cut on it: *I loved her as a maiden; I will not trouble Erlend's
detestable wife; better she should be a widow.*

Words scored upon a bone,
Scratched in despair or rage—
Nine hundred years have gone;
Now, in another age,
They burn with passion on
A scholar's tranquil page.

The scholar takes his pen
And turns the bone about,
And writes those words again.
Once more they seethe and shout,
And through a human brain
Undying hate rings out.

"I loved her when a maid;
I loathe and love the wife
That warms another's bed:
Let him beware his life!"
The scholar's hand is stayed;
His pen becomes a knife

To grave in living bone
The fierce archaic cry.
He sits and reads his own
Dull sum of misery.
A thousand years have flown
Before that ink is dry.

And, in a foreign tongue,
A man, who is not he,

Reads and his heart is wrung
This ancient grief to see,
And thinks: When I am dung,
What bone shall speak for me?

A. D. Hope

'DO NOT GO GENTLE INTO THAT GOOD NIGHT'

Do not go gentle into that good night,
Old age should burn and rave at close of day;
Rage, rage against the dying of the light.

Though wise men at their end know dark is right,
Because their words had forked no lightning they
Do not go gentle into that good night.

Good men, the last wave by, crying how bright
Their frail deeds might have danced in a green bay,
Rage, rage against the dying of the light.

Wild men who caught and sang the sun in flight,
And learn, too late, they grieved it on its way,
Do not go gentle into that good night.

Grave men, near death, who see with blinding sight
Blind eyes could blaze like meteors and be gay,
Rage, rage against the dying of the light.

And you, my father, there on the sad height,
Curse, bless, me now with your fierce tears, I pray.
Do not go gentle into that good night.
Rage, rage against the dying of the light.

Dylan Thomas

II.

NEAREST
BUT
NOT DEAREST

The bitterest hatred is the hatred of close relatives.

TACITUS, *History*

Lizzie Borden took an ax
And gave her mother forty whacks.
When she saw what she had done
She gave her father forty-one.

American popular verse, ca. 1895

[LEAR'S CURSE ON GONERIL]

Hear, nature, hear; dear goddess, hear!
Suspend thy purpose, if thou didst intend
To make this creature fruitful:
Into her womb convey sterility,
Dry up in her the organs of increase,
And from her derogate body never spring
A babe to honor her! If she must teem,
Create her child of spleen, that it may live
And be a thwart disnatured torment to her.
Let it stamp wrinkles in her brow of youth;
With cadent¹ tears fret channels in her cheeks;
Turn all her mother's pains and benefits
To laughter and contempt, that she may feel
How sharper than a serpent's tooth it is
To have a thankless child! Away, away!

William Shakespeare
King Lear, I, iv

1. *cadent:* falling

[THE CENCI'S CURSE UPON HIS DAUGHTER]

   Lucretia.   She said, 'I cannot come;
Go tell my father, that I see a torrent
Of his own blood raging between us.'
   Cenci (kneeling).   God!
Hear me! If this most specious mass of flesh,
Which Thou hast made my daughter; this my blood,
This particle of my divided being;
Or rather, this my bane and my disease,
Whose sight infects and poisons me; this devil
Which sprung from me as from a hell, was meant

To aught good use; if her bright loveliness
Was kindled to illumine this dark world;
If nursed by Thy selectest dew of love
Such virtues blossom in her as should make
The peace of life, I pray Thee for my sake,
As Thou the common God and Father art
Of her, and me, and all; reverse that doom!
Earth, in the name of God, let her food be
Poison, until she be encrusted round
With leprous stains! Heaven, rain upon her head
The blistering drops of the Maremma's dew,
Till she be speckled like a toad; parch up
Those love-enkindled lips, warp those fine limbs
To loathèd lameness! All-beholding sun,
Strike in thine envy those life-darting eyes
With thine own blinding beams!
    Lucretia.   Peace! Peace!
For thine own sake unsay those dreadful words.
When high God grants He punishes such prayers.
    Cenci (leaping up, and throwing his right hand towards Heaven).
      He does His will, I mine! This in addition,
That if she have a child . . .
    Lucretia.   Horrible thought!
    Cenci.   That if she ever have a child; and thou,
Quick Nature! I adjure thee by thy God,
That thou be fruitful in her, and increase
And multiply, fulfilling his command,
And my deep imprecation! May it be
A hideous likeness of herself, that as
From a distorting mirror, she may see
Her image mixed with what she most abhors,
Smiling upon her from her nursing breast.
And that the child may from its infancy
Grow, day by day, more wicked and deformed,

Turning her mother's love to misery:
And that both she and it may live until
It shall repay her care and pain with hate,
Or what may else be more unnatural.
So he may hunt her through the clamorous scoffs
Of the loud world to a dishonoured grave.
Shall I revoke this curse? Go, bid her come,
Before my words are chronicled in Heaven.

[*Exit* LUCRETIA.

I do not feel as if I were a man,
But like a fiend appointed to chastise
The offences of some unremembered world.
My blood is running up and down my veins;
A fearful pleasure makes it prick and tingle:
I feel a giddy sickness of strange awe;
My heart is beating with an expectation
Of horrid joy.

Percy Bysshe Shelley
The Cenci, IV, i

INHERITANCE*

Three things seek my death,
    Hard at my heels they run—
Hang them, sweet Christ, all three,
    Devil, maggot and son.

Each of them only craves
    The morsel that falls to his share,
And cares not a thrauneen what
    Falls to the other pair.

The spirit of guilt and guile
        Would compound for my soul in sin
And leave my flesh to the worm,
        My money to my kin.

My sons think more of the gold
        That will come to them when I die
Than a soul they could not spend,
        A body that none would buy.

And how would the maggot fare
        On a soul too thin to eat
And money too tough to chew?
        He must have my body for meat.

Christ speared by the blind man,
        Christ nailed to a naked tree,
The three that seek my end,
        Hang them, sweet Christ, all three.

Frank O'Connor

DADDY*

You do not do, you do not do
Any more, black shoe
In which I have lived like a foot
For thirty years, poor and white,
Barely daring to breathe or Achoo.

Daddy, I have had to kill you.
You died before I had time————
Marble-heavy, a bag full of God,

Ghastly statue with one grey toe
Big as a Frisco seal

And a head in the freakish Atlantic
Where it pours bean green over blue
In the waters off beautiful Nauset.
I used to pray to recover you.
Ach, du.

In the German tongue, in the Polish town
Scraped flat by the roller
Of wars, wars, wars.
But the name of the town is common.
My Polack friend

Says there are a dozen or two.
So I never could tell where you
Put your foot, your root,
I never could talk to you.
The tongue stuck in my jaw.

It stuck in a barb wire snare.
Ich, ich, ich, ich,
I could hardly speak.
I thought every German was you.
And the language obscene

An engine, an engine
Chuffing me off like a Jew.
A Jew to Dachau, Auschwitz, Belsen.
I began to talk like a Jew.
I think I may well be a Jew.

The snows of the Tyrol, the clear beer of Vienna
Are not very pure or true.
With my gypsy ancestress and my weird luck
And my Taroc pack and my Taroc pack
I may be a bit of a Jew.

I have always been scared of *you*,
With your Luftwaffe, your gobbledygoo.
And your neat moustache
And your Aryan eye, bright blue.
Panzer-man, panzer-man, O You————

Not God but a swastika
So black no sky could squeak through.
Every woman adores a Fascist,
The boot in the face, the brute
Brute heart of a brute like you.

You stand at the blackboard, daddy,
In the picture I have of you,
A cleft in your chin instead of your foot
But no less a devil for that, no not
Any less the black man who

Bit my pretty red heart in two.
I was ten when they buried you.
At twenty I tried to die
And get back, back, back to you.
I thought even the bones would do.

But they pulled me out of the sack,
And they stuck me together with glue.
And then I knew what to do.

I made a model of you,
A man in black with a Meinkampf look

And a love of the rack and the screw.
And I said I do, I do.
So daddy, I'm finally through.
The black telephone's off at the root,
The voices just can't worm through.

If I've killed one man, I've killed two———
The vampire who said he was you
And drank my blood for a year,
Seven years, if you want to know.
Daddy, you can lie back now.

There's a stake in your fat black heart
And the villagers never liked you.
They are dancing and stamping on you.
They always *knew* it was you.
Daddy, daddy, you bastard, I'm through.

Sylvia Plath

BONA DE MORTUIS

Aye, the good man, kind father, best of friends—
These are the words that grow like grass and nettles
Out of dead men, and speckled hatreds hide
Like toads among them.

Thomas Lovell Beddoes

EDWARD

"Why dois your brand[1] sae drap wi' bluid,
  Edward, Edward?
Why dois your brand sae drap wi' bluid?
  And why sae said gang ye, O?"
"O, I hae killed my hauke sae guid,
  Mither, mither,
O, I hae killed my hauke sae guid,
  And I had nae mair but he, O."

"Your haukis bluid was nevir sae reid,
  Edward, Edward,
Your haukis bluid was nevir sae reid,
  My deir son I tell thee, O."
"O, I hae killed my reid-roan steid,
  Mither, mither,
O, I hae killed my reid-roan steid,
  That erst was sa fair and free, O."

"Your steid was auld, and ye hae gat mair,
  Edward, Edward,
Your steid was auld, and ye hae gat mair,
  Sum other dule ye drie,[2] O."
"O, I hae killed my fadir deir,
  Mither, mither,
O, I hae killed my fadir deir,
  Alas, and wae is me, O!"

"And whatten penance wul ye drie for that,
  Edward, Edward?
And whatten penance will ye drie for that?
  My deir son, now tell me, O."
"Ile set my feit in yonder boat,

Mither, mither,
Ile set my feit in yonder boat,
And Ile fare ovir the sea, O."

"And what wul ye do wi' your towirs and your ha',
Edward, Edward,
And what wul ye do wi' your towirs and your ha',
That were sae fair to see, O?"
"Ile let thame stand tul they doun fa',
Mither, mither,
Ile let thame stand tul they doun fa',
For here nevir mair maun I be, O."

"And what wul ye leive to your bairns and your wife,
Edward, Edward?
And what wul ye leive to your bairns and your wife,
When ye gang ovir the sea, O?"
"The warldis room, let them beg thrae life,
Mither, mither,
The warldis room, let them beg thrae life,
For thame nevir mair wul I see, O."

"And what wul ye leive to your ain mither deir,
Edward, Edward?
And what wul ye leive to your ain mither deir?
My deir son, now tell me, O."
"The curse of Hell frae me sall ye beir,
Mither, mither,
The curse of Hell frae me sall ye beir,
Sic counseils ye gave to me, O."

Anonymous
traditional Scottish ballad

1. *brand:* sword. 2. *dule ye drie:* sorrow you suffer.

REVENGE FABLE

There was a person
Could not get rid of his mother
As if he were her topmost twig.
So he pounded and hacked at her
With numbers and equations and laws
Which he invented and called truth.
He investigated, incriminated
And penalized her, like Tolstoy,
Forbidding, screaming and condemning,
Going for her with a knife,
Obliterating her with disgusts
Bulldozers and detergents
Requisitions and central heating
Rifles and whisky and bored sleep.

With all her babes in her arms, in ghostly weepings,
She died.

His head fell off like a leaf.

Ted Hughes
Crow

FOR AN OBLIGATE PARASITE

Mother!, I am sick
of alcohol and grown up
foods. That blue milk
diet that I used to suck
is what I need. If you
give up your sour weeds

I will tear out
my permanently biting teeth
so we can be attached
again as sucker-shark
and shark, I mouthless on
you, and you savagely mouthed.
Oh we will course the Deeps
as pure efficiencies
where life obeys its first
imperative of desire: eat!,
and not the second: screw!
Oh I will close my eyes
so tight they disappear
in trusting sleep: who needs
them? Wills. Lovers. You.

Alan Dugan

GENITORI

And we are the commotion born of love.
—CHARLES MADGE

As a Buddhist tried for months
To visualize a small gold Bodhissatva on the air,
I benignly conjure up this couple,
His arms about her, free of trouble.
They're young and smiling, apple clean,
Whose embraces gave my shining hair,
And she is both his piano and his cello,
Which are played with fingers, light
Arpeggios now and then, rough gutsy
Rubbing of the belly when it's night
And how well I know, in cold December,
The poor lived better, in glowing embers

Of their kindling crates, than we did
Wrapped in our clawed-up gramma's quilts.
In the decades later they still obsess us
So that daily we forgive them and daily
Don't, and in a field may find them still,
Blue in paired flowers, their love transposed
And borne beyond a billion rocks, and time,
Or caught within a cave by those
Who knew them before us, suffering sister,
Who wept in the Oklahoma night.
Their best and worst I sing, no longer hate.
And I smile to see my mother still,
Cradling the steaming soup, straight down
The hill, to those wretched poor who huddled there
While we at home, brother, sister, sucked the bloody air.

David Ray

CONFESSION TO SETTLE A CURSE

You don't
know
who I am
because
you don't know
my mother
she's always been an exemplary mother
told me so herself
there were reasons she
had to lock
everything that could be locked
there's much can be
locked

in a good German household crowded
with wardrobes dressers sideboards
bookcases cupboards chests bureaus
desks trunks caskets coffers all with lock
and key
and locked
it was lots of trouble
for her
just carry that enormous key ring
be bothered all the time
I wanted scissors stationery
my winter coat and she had to unlock
the drawer get it out and lock
all up again
me she reproached for lacking
confidence not being open
I have a mother I can tell everything
she told me so
I've
been bound
made fast
locked
by the key witch
but a small
winner
I'm not
in turn locking
a child
in my arms

Rosmarie Waldrop

THE WHIPPING

The old woman across the way
   is whipping the boy again
and shouting to the neighborhood
   her goodness and his wrongs.

Wildly he crashes through elephant ears,
   pleads in dusty zinnias,
while she in spite of crippling fat
   pursues and corners him.

She strikes and strikes the shrilly circling
   boy till the stick breaks
in her hand. His tears are rainy weather
   to woundlike memories:

My head gripped in bony vise
   of knees, the writhing struggle
to wrench free, the blows, the fear
   worse than blows that hateful

Words could bring, the face that I
   no longer knew or loved . . .
Well, it is over now, it is over,
   and the boy sobs in his room,

And the woman leans muttering against
   a tree, exhausted, purged—
avenged in part for lifelong hidings
   she has had to bear.

Robert Hayden

CENSORSHIP

Damn that celibate farm, that cracker-box house
with the bed springs screaming at every stir,
even to breathe. I swear, if one of us
half turned they'd shriek, "He's getting on top of her!"

Her father, but for the marriage certificate,
would have his .30-.30 up my ass.
Her mother, certificate or not, could hate
a hole right through the wall. It was

a banshee's way to primroses that fall
of the first year in that hate-bed wired
like a burglar alarm. If I stood her against the wall,
that would quiver and creak. When we got tired

of the dog-humped floor we sneaked out for a stroll
and tumbled it out under the apple tree
just up from the spring, but the chiggers ate us whole
in that locked conspiracy of chastity

whose belts we both wore all one grated week
while virtue buzzed a blue-fly over that bitch
of a bed hair-triggered to shriek:
"They're going at it! They're doing it right now!"—which

we damned well couldn't, welted over and on
as if we were sunburned. And every night at two
her mother would get up and go to the john,
and the plumbing would howl from Hell, "We're
     watching you!"

                                        John Ciardi

THE BROTHER-IN-LAW

Haunt him, Mona! Haunt him, demon sister!
He who filled your bed for twenty years,
Inflating placentas, till you withered in
His bursting gifts, and burrowed into safer
Ground, he will betray those nights; he's found
A woman newer in the flesh, and has pushed
Your grave below his bed.
                              They will wed,
But I who was your lover first, before
I knew what women hid—by the manhood
I had then, I conjure you to wall
Their nights, and lie between their straining parts.
Haunt him in his massive hour—
                              child, I call.

Larry Rubin

BYE BABY BOTHER

Bye Baby Bother
Where is your brother?

They so-and-so and so-and-so
And twisted his guts
In a nasty way
Because he said they were nuts.

Bye Baby Bother
How shall I keep them from your pother?

I will be quiet now, Mother, but when there is a general
    mobilization
Dozens of chaps like me will know what to do with our
    ammunition.

Dozens by hundreds will be taken and torn,
Oh would the day had died first when you were born.

Stevie Smith

III.

SEXUAL
SKIRMISHES

Oh, do not die, for I shall hate
All women so when thou art gone.
JOHN DONNE, "The Fever"

Snips and snails and puppydog tails,
That's what little boys are made of.
English nursery rhyme

He's an ugly body, a bubbly body,
An ill-fared hideous loon,
And I have married a keelman,
And my good days are done!
"The Sandgate Girl's Lamentation,"
broadside ballad

And eek I praye Jhesu shorte hir lyves
That wol nat be governed by hir wyves;
And olde and angry nygardes of dispence,
God sende hem soone verray pestilence!
THE WIFE OF BATH
in Chaucer's *Canterbury Tales*

'I MARRIED IN MY YOUTH A WIFE'

I married in my youth a wife.
She was my own, my very first.
She gave the best years of her life.
I hope nobody gets the worst.

                                    J. V. Cunningham

NERVOUS PROSTRATION

I married a man of the Croydon class
When I was twenty-two.
And I vex him, and he bores me
Till we don't know what to do!
It isn't good form in the Croydon class
To say you love your wife,
So I spend my days with the tradesmen's books
And pray for the end of life.

In green fields are blossoming trees
And a golden wealth of gorse,
And young birds sing for joy of worms:
It's perfectly clear, of course,
That it wouldn't be taste in the Croydon class
To sing over dinner or tea:
But I sometimes wish the gentleman
Would turn and talk to me!

But every man of the Croydon class
Lives in terror of joy and speech,
"Words are betrayers," "Joys are brief"
The maxims their wise ones teach.

And for all my labour of love and life
I shall be clothed and fed,
And they'll give me an orderly funeral
When I'm still enough to be dead.

I married a man of the Croydon class
When I was twenty-two.
And I vex him, and he bores me
Till we don't know what to do!
And as I sit in his ordered house,
I feel I must sob or shriek,
To force a man of the Croydon class
To live, or to love, or to speak!

Anna Wickham

THE BROCKTON MURDER:
A PAGE OUT OF WILLIAM JAMES*

Bored with his wife that fatal day
—said the villain of the 'Brockton murder'—
he fired four shots. The woman lay
scarcely alive, but her husband heard her.

'You didn't do it on purpose, dear?'
'No, I didn't,' the husband said.
However (making his meaning clear)
he found a rock and smashed her head.

Though William James described this crime
to illustrate his view of chance,
the woman's question every time
absorbs the murder's relevance.

Knute Skinner

BLANK VERSE FOR A FAT DEMANDING WIFE

As I roll back from you,
from your flabby breasts and breath,
a faint froth is our only link.

How many beaches are you?
Must I comb them all?

I'm not a wave to roll again forever,
and unlike the sea,
I don't come
every fifteen seconds.

Jim Lindsey

YOU FIT INTO ME

you fit into me
like a hook into an eye

a fish hook
an open eye

Margaret Atwood

A LADY

"Asshole" and "shit" were always on her lips;
    What other joys she sought mostly were oral.
        As she came puckering toward me, I advanced,

Then bent and kissed each of her fingertips,
Well satisfied. It isn't that I'm moral
   Or elegant: I know she wipes her hands.

W. D. Snodgrass

THE DEAD BRIDE

So white I was, he would have me cry
   'Unclean!' murderously
To heal me with far-fetched blood.

I writhed to conceive of him.
I clawed to becalm him.
Some nights, I witnessed his face in sleep

And dreamed of my father's
House. (By day he professed languages—
   Disciplines of languages)—

By day I cleansed my pink tongue
From its nightly prowl, its vixen-skill,
   His sacramental mouth

   That justified my flesh
And moved well among women
In nuances and imperatives.

This was the poet of a people's
   Love. I hated him. He weeps,
Solemnizing his loss.

Geoffrey Hill

THE SILLY OLD MAN

Come listen awhile, and I'll sing you a song:
I am a young damsel just turned twenty-one.
I married a miser for gold, it is true,
And the age of his years were seventy-two.

[*Chorus:*]

Will you live for ever, you silly old man?
I wish that your days they were all at an end!
To please a young woman is more than you can—
It's not in your power, you silly old man.

For every night when I go to bed
He lays by my side like one that is dead.
Such spitting and coughing, it makes me run wild,
Though I'm never disturbed by the noise of my child.

Was there ever a woman so sorely oppressed,
For every morning I've got him for to dress,
And like a young child I have got him for to nusse,
For he's got ne'er a tooth to mumble a crust.

When I go to bed to him he makes me run wild,
For he's got no more use in his limbs than a child,
He feels all as cold as a piece of lead,
That I have a great mind to get out of bed.

There's a buxom young fellow that lives in this town
That pleases me well, so we'll cut out the clown.
I'll make him wear horns as long as a stag,
So we'll cuckold the miser and seize his gold bag.

When I go to bed to him I do not lay nigh,

For he grunts and he groans like a pig in a sty.
I'm sure a young woman would soon wish him dead,
He's as bald as a coot with no teeth in his head.

Will you live for ever, you silly old man?
I wish that your days they were all at an end!
I'll spend all your gold with some lusty young man—
So go to your grave, you silly old man.

Anonymous
English broadside ballad, nineteenth century

LOVE LETTER

For months now you've hated me
    and sent on angry letters
From creditors without comment
    though you've had to address
New envelopes; your anger
    is joined to theirs
And I take it all broadside
    here in an empty apartment
Where I watch the cars plunge
    past all night, where I own
A morning moon above distant farms
    and my cough annoys no one.

David Ray

THE GLUTTON

Beyond the Atlas roams a glutton
Lusty and sleek, a shameless robber,
Sacred to Aethiopian Aphrodite;

The aborigines harry it with darts,
And its flesh is esteemed, though of a fishy tang
Tainting the eater's mouth and lips.

Ourselves once, wandering in mid-wilderness
And by despair drawn to this diet,
Before the meal was over sat apart
Loathing each other's carrion company.

Robert Graves

THE LONELINESS OF
THE LONG DISTANCE RUNNER

My wife bursts into the room
where I'm writing well
of my love for her

and because now
the poem is lost

I silently curse her.

Alden Nowlan

THE COUPLE OVERHEAD

They don't get anywhere,
The couple overhead;
They wrangle like the damned
In the bed above my bed,
But the harm has all been done.
And this is a short despair:
Count Ugolino dead

Was endlessly condemned
To gnaw the archbishop's head
Where the nape and the skull are one.

Not so, these secular drunks.
Dante would find their treason
Too spiritless to keep;
Like children stealing raisins
They eat each other's eyes;
The ice that grips their flanks
Is something they have frozen.
After a while they sleep;
And the punishment they've chosen,
After a while it dies.

William Meredith

UPON SCOBBLE*

Scobble for whoredom whips his wife, and cries
He'll slit her nose; but blubbering she replies,
Good Sir, make no more cuts i'th'outward skin,
One slit's enough to let Adultery in.

Robert Herrick

AN OLD MALEDICTION

freely from Horace

What well-heeled knuckle-head, straight from the unisex
Hairstylist and bathed in *Russian Leather*,
Dallies with you these late summer days, Pyrrha,

In your expensive sublet? For whom do you
Slip into something simple by, say, Gucci?
The more fool he who has mapped out for himself
The saline latitudes of incontinent grief.
Dazzled though he be, poor dope, by the golden looks
Your locks fetched up out of a bottle of *Clairol*,
He will know that the wind changes, the smooth sailing
Is done for, when the breakers wallop him broadside,
When he's rudderless, dismasted, thoroughly swamped
In that mindless rip-tide that got the best of me
Once, when I ventured on your deeps, Piranha.

Anthony Hecht

THE CURSE

Whoever guesses, thinks, or dreams he knows
Who is my mistress, wither by this curse:
    His only, and only his purse
    May some dull heart to love dispose,
And she yield then to all that are his foes;
    May he be scorned by one, whom all else scorn,
    Forswear to others, what to her he hath sworn,
    With fear of missing, shame of getting, torn:

Madness his sorrow, gout his cramp, may he
Make by but thinking who hath made him such:
    And may he feel no touch
    Of conscience, but of fame, and be
Anguished, not that 'twas sin, but that 'twas she:
    In early and long scarceness may he rot,
    For land which had been his, if he had not
    Himself incestuously an heir begot:

May he dream treason, and believe that he
Meant to perform it, and confess, and die,
    And no record tell why:
    His sons, which none of his may be,
Inherit nothing but his infamy:
    Or may he so long parasites have fed,
    That he would fain be theirs, whom he hath bred.
    And at the last be circumcised for bread:

The venom of all stepdames, gamesters' gall,
What tyrants and their subjects interwish,
    What plants, mines, beasts, fowl, fish
    Can contribute, all ill which all
Prophets or poets spake; and all which shall
    Be annexed in schedules unto this by me,
    Fall on that man; for if it be a she,
    Nature beforehand hath out-cursèd me.

John Donne

SONG

    Love a woman? You're an ass!
      'Tis a most insipid passion
    To choose out for your happiness
      The silliest part of God's creation.

    Let the porter and the groom,
      Things designed for dirty slaves,
    Drudge in fair Aurelia's womb
      To get supplies for age and graves.

Farewell, woman! I intend
　Henceforth every night to sit
With my lewd, well-natured friend,
　Drinking to engender wit.

Then give me health, wealth, mirth, and wine,
　And, if busy love entrenches,
There's a sweet, soft page of mine
　Does the trick worth forty wenches.

John Wilmot, Earl of Rochester

FINGER OF NECESSITY

Postal Area #29, Los Angeles

Twice recently young girls have
　　given me the finger. The
　first was on the freeway, she

sitting close to her boyfriend turned
　　with sure purpose and aimed
　at prominence, seatbelted in

two lanes over. The chemical shock to
　　my system made me feel so
　like they wanted I chased them

for miles trying to think of something
　　to yell back. The second a few
　minutes ago standing beside a

drugstore would have been easy to

go back by but I just waved
like oh another one. It must

be something in the atmosphere, Scorpio
on the ascendant, or maybe they
were bored with the just looking

and better this than what I didn't give,
much better. With one buzzoff
finger she became the mother

of my invention with her red
shirt and her hiphuggers
and her flowered vinyl belt:

Hey cat lady, you eat it.

Coleman Barks

TRIOLET

All women born are so perverse
No man need boast their love possessing.
If nought seem better, nothing's worse:
All women born are so perverse.
From Adam's wife, that proved a curse
Though God had made her for a blessing,
All women born are so perverse
No man need boast their love possessing.

Robert Bridges

THE RAPER FROM PASSENACK

was very kind. When she regained
her wits, he said, It's all right, kid,
I took care of you.

What a mess she was in. Then he added,
You'll never forget me now.
And drove her home.

Only a man who is sick, she said
would do a thing like that.
It must be so.

No one who is not diseased could be
so insanely cruel. He wants to give it
to someone else—

to justify himself. But if I get a
venereal infection out of this
I won't be treated.

I refuse. You'll find me dead in bed
first. Why not? That's
the way she spoke,

I wish I could shoot him. How would
you like to know a murderer?
I may do it.

I'll know by the end of this week.
I wouldn't scream. I bit him
several times

but he was too strong for me.
I can't yet understand it. I don't
faint so easily.

When I came to myself and realized
what had happened all I could do
was to curse

and call him every vile name I could
think of. I was so glad
to be taken home.

I suppose it's my mind—the fear of
infection. I'd rather a million times
have been got pregnant.

But it's the foulness of it can't
be cured. And hatred, hatred of all men
—and disgust.

William Carlos Williams

THE OBSCENE CALLER

He breathes into my earpiece late at night.
Softly and surprisingly dry, he pushes me
Open like a baby branch, excited by the chance he's taking.
His voice balances me on thin wire.
His shoddy eye imagines how I lie in my bed,
Transports it to his own which is next to the phone,
And binding my legs with the cord
He presses down on my face
Ringing again and again.

Cheri Fein

I DON'T HAVE NO BUNNY TAIL ON MY BEHIND

i don't have no bunny tail on my behind.
i'm a sister of the blood taboo.

my throat's too tight to swallow.
must be because i'm scared to death. i'm scared to live.
how do i get thru the day? the night?
guts, fella. that's how

what are your perversions to me?
what do i care you want sadistic broads in black boots,
cigarettes up your asshole?
what do i care?
that's our child sleeping in that blue crib

how did it feel:
that cigarette up my nose?
how did it feel?
you grimacing "does it hurt, baby? does it hurt?"
how did it feel to curse your pretty smile,
pray blindness strike your ice blue eyes?
how did it feel to curse: may you never know joy.
i hate your very soul.

i swore to avenge all the wasted dead, the caged wives.
what vengeance could answer our pain, our fury?
i hope i find out before i die.
in my cunt is blood & i always want it to be your blood.
i hope you bleed 5 days every month. i hope your strength
    drains down the toilet.

you're afraid of me.
you laugh. you hit me.
you're running scared, man.
our voodoo dolls are all worn out.

yes i hate you.
yes i want your cock

off.
yes i want your blood & balls to spill
like my monthly payment in blood.
yes i want you to beat off in shame,
afraid to call me.
yes i want you dead.
when i was married i prayed to be a widow.
there are still wives. they are still preying.

yes i want you to flinch when i laugh
flinch when i laugh
my teeth tearing your heart, knowing your love is poisoned,
you cannot wash clean,
knowing the earth & i will outlive you.
you are a dying breed, you & your penis guns,
your joyless fucks, you are dying,
you are dying,
the curse of every wicked witch be upon your heart.
i could not hate you more if hatred were my bones.

Alta

TO HELL WITH YOUR FERTILITY CULT

To hell with your Fertility Cult, I
never did want to be fertile,
you think this world is just
a goddamn oversize cunt, don't you? Everything
crowding in and out of it like a railway
terminal   and isn't that nice?
all those people going on trips.
well this is what it feels like, she said,
—and knocked the hen off the nest, grabbed
an egg and threw it at him, right in the face,
the half-formed chick half clung, half slid
half-alive, down over his cheekbone, around
the corner of his mouth, part of it thick
yellow and faintly visible bones and it drippt
down his cheek and chin
—he had nothing to say.

Gary Snyder

THE LADY'S-MAID'S SONG*

for *The Man of Mode*

When Adam found his rib was gone
    He cursed and sighed and cried and swore
And looked with cold resentment on
    The creature God had used it for.
All love's delights were quickly spent
    And soon his sorrows multiplied:
He learned to blame his discontent
    On something stolen from his side.

And so in every age we find
    Each Jack, destroying every Joan,
Divides and conquers womankind
    In vengeance for his missing bone.
By day he spins out quaint conceits
    With gossip, flattery, and song,
But then at night, between the sheets,
    He wrongs the girl to right the wrong.

Though shoulder, bosom, lip, and knee
    Are praised in every kind of art,
Here is love's true anatomy:
    His rib is gone; he'll have her heart.
So women bear the debt alone
    And live eternally distressed,
For though we throw the dog his bone
    He wants it back with interest.

John Hollander

IV.

PERSONAL ANIMOSITIES

I do not like thee, Doctor Fell,
The reason why I cannot tell,
But this I know and know full well,
I do not like thee, Doctor Fell.
THOMAS BROWN, 1678, after Martial*

A petty sneaking knave I knew—
O Mr. Cromek, how do ye do?
WILLIAM BLAKE

LAW IN THE COUNTRY OF THE CATS

When two men meet for the first time in all
Eternity and outright hate each other,
Not as a beggar-man and a rich man,
Not as cuckold-maker and cuckold,
Not as bully and delicate boy, but
As dog and wolf because their blood before
They are aware has bristled into their hackles,
Because one has clubbed the other to death
With the bottle first broached to toast their transaction
And swears to God he went helpless black-out
While they were mixing smiles, facts have sacked
The oath of the pious witness who judged all men
As a one humble brotherhood of man.

When two men at first meeting hate each other
Even in passing, without words, in the street,
They are not likely to halt as if remembering
They once met somewhere, where in fact they met,
And discuss "universal brotherhood,"
"Love of humanity and each fellow-man,"
Or "the growing likelihood of perpetual peace,"
But if, by chance, they do meet, so mistaking,
There will be that moment's horrible pause
As each looks into the gulf in the eye of the other,
Then a flash of violent incredible action,
Then one man letting his brains gently to the gutter,
And one man bursting into the police station
Crying: "Let Justice be done. I did it, I."

Ted Hughes

WILLY WET-LEG

I can't stand Willy wet-leg,
can't stand him at any price.
He's resigned, and when you hit him
he lets you hit him twice.

D. H. *Lawrence*

DICK, A MAGGOT

As when rooting in a bin,
All powdered o'er from tail to chin,
A lively maggot sallies out,
You know him by his hazel snout:
So, when the grandson of his grandsire,
Forth issues wriggling Dick Drawcensir
With powdered rump and back and side,
You cannot blanch his tawny hide;
For 'tis beyond the pow'r of meal
The gipsy visage to conceal:
For, as he shakes his wainscot chops,
Down ev'ry mealy atom drops
And leaves the Tartar phiz, in show
Like a fresh turd just dropped on snow.

Jonathan Swift

A SONG*

Good neighbour, why do you look awry?
  You are a wond'rous stranger:
You walk about, you huff and pout
  As if you'd burst with anger.

Is it for that your fortune's great,
  Or you so wealthy are,
Or live so high there's none a-nigh
  That can with you compare?
But t'other day I heard one say
  Your husband durst not show his ears,
But like a lout does walk about
  So full of sighs and fears.
Good Mrs. Tart, I caren't a fart
  For you nor all your jeers.

My husband's known for to be one
  That is most chaste and pure,
And so would be continually
  But for such jades as you are:
You wash, you lick, you smug, you trick,
  You toss a twire,[1] a grin;
You nod and wink, and in his drink,
  You strive to draw him in;
You lie, you punk; you're always drunk;
  Now you scold and make a strife,
And like a whore you run o' the score
  And lead him a weary life.
Tell me so again, you dirty queen,
  And I'll pull you by the quoif![2]

Go dress those brats, those nasty rats,
  That have a leer so drowsy;
With vermin spread they look like dead,
  Good faith, they're always lousy!
Pray hold you there and do not swear,
  You are not half so sweet;
You feed yours up with bit and sup
  And give them a dirty teat.
My girls, my boys, my only joys

Are better fed and taught than yours;
You lie, you flirt; you look like dirt,
  I'll kick you out of doors!
A very good jest, pray do your best,
  And faith, I'll quit your scores.

Go, go! you are a nasty bear,
  Your husband cannot bear it;
A nasty queen as e'er was seen,
  Your neighbours all can swear it:
A fulsome trot³ and good for nought
  Unless it be to chat;
You stole a spoon out of the room,
  Last christ'ning you were at;
You lie, you bitch; you've got the itch,
  Your neighbours know you're not sound—
Look how you claw with your nasty paw!
  And I'll fell you to the ground;
You've tore my hood, you shall make it good
  If it cost me forty pound!

Anonymous
English popular ballad, late seventeenth century

1. *twire:* a leering glance. 2. *quoif:* coif, close-fitting cap. 3. *trot:* loafer.

'WHEN SIR JOSHUA REYNOLDS DIED'*

When Sir Joshua Reynolds died
All Nature was degraded;
The King dropped a tear into the Queen's ear
And all his pictures faded.

William Blake

[SPORUS]

Let Sporus[1] tremble—"What? that thing of silk,
Sporus, that mere white curd of ass's milk?
Satire or sense, alas, can Sporus feel?
Who breaks a butterfly upon a wheel?"
Yet let me flap this bug with gilded wings,
This painted child of dirt that stinks and stings;
Whose buzz the witty and the fair annoys,
Yet wit ne'er tastes, and beauty ne'er enjoys,
So well-bred spaniels civilly delight
In mumbling of the game they dare not bite.
Eternal smiles his emptiness betray,
As shallow streams run dimpling all the way.
Whether in florid impotence he speaks,
And, as the prompter breathes, the puppet squeaks;
Or at the ear of Eve, familiar toad,
Half froth, half venom, spits himself abroad
In puns or politics, or tales or lies,
Or spite, or smut, or rhymes, or blasphemies;
His wit all see-saw between *that* and *this*,
Now high, now low, now master up, now miss,
And he himself one vile antithesis.
Amphibious thing! that acting either part,
The trifling head, or the corrupted heart!
Fop at the toilet, flatterer at the board,
Now trips a lady, and now struts a lord.
Eve's tempter thus the Rabbins have expressed,
A cherub's face, a reptile all the rest;
Beauty that shocks you, parts that none will trust,
Wit that can creep, and pride that licks the dust.

Alexander Pope
An Epistle from Mr. Pope to Dr. Arbuthnot

1. *Sporus:* Lord Hervey.

THE PLAYBOY OF THE DEMI-WORLD: 1938

Aloft in Heavenly Mansions, Doubleyou One—
Just Mayfair flats, but certainly sublime—
You'll find the abode of D'Arcy Honeybunn,
A rose-red cissy half as old as time.

Peace cannot age him, and no war could kill
The genial tenant of those cosy rooms,
He's lived there always and he lives there still,
Perennial pansy, hardiest of blooms.

There you'll encounter aunts of either sex,
Their jokes equivocal or over-ripe,
Ambiguous couples wearing slacks and specs
And the stout Lesbian knocking out her pipe.

The rooms are crammed with flowers and *objets d'art*,
A Ganymede still hands the drinks—and plenty!
D'Arcy still keeps a rakish-looking car
And still behaves the way he did at twenty.

A ruby pin is fastened in his tie,
The scent he uses is *Adieu Sagesse*.
His shoes are suede, and as the years go by
His tailor's bill's not getting any less.

He cannot whistle, always rises late,
Is good at indoor sports and parlor-tricks,
Mauve is his favorite color, and his gait
Suggests a pea-hen walking on hot bricks.

He prances forward with his hands outspread
And folds all comers in a gay embrace,

A wavy toupee on his hairless head,
A fixed smile on his often-lifted face.

'My dears!' he lisps, to whom all men are dear,
'How perfectly enchanting of you!'; turns
Towards his guests and twitters, 'Look who's here!
Do come and help us fiddle while Rome burns!'

'The kindest man alive,' so people say,
'Perpetual youth!' 'But have you seen his eyes?'
The eyes of some old saurian in decay
That asks no questions and is told no lies.

Under the fribble lurks a worn-out sage
Heavy with disillusion, and alone;
So never say to D'Arcy, 'Be your age!'—
He'd shrivel up at once or turn to stone.

William Plomer

LINES FOR A CHRISTMAS CARD

May all my enemies go to hell,
Noel, Noel, Noel, Noel.

Hilaire Belloc

BLACK BULL OF ALDGATE*

Black Bull of Aldgate, may thy horns rot from the sockets!
For, jingling threepence, porter's pay, in hungry pockets,
And thirty times at least beneath thy doorway stepping

I've waited for this lousy coach that runs to Epping.
Ill luck befall thee, that hast made me so splenetic,
Through all thy holes and closets up from tap to attic,
Through all thy boys and bootses, chambermaids, and waiters,
And yonder booking-office-clerk in fustian gaiters.
Black Bull of Aldgate! mayst thou more miscarry
Than ever hasty Clement's did with bloated Harry!

Alfred, Lord Tennyson

I WISH MY TONGUE WERE A QUIVER*

I wish my tongue were a quiver the size of a huge cask
Packed and crammed with long black venomous rankling darts.
I'd fling you more full of them, and joy in the task,
Than ever Sebastian was, or Caesar, with thirty-three swords
    in his heart.

I'd make a porcupine out of you, or a pincushion, say;
The shafts should stand so thick you'd look like a headless hen
Hung up by the heels, with the long bare red neck stretching,
    curving, and dripping away
From the soiled floppy ball of ruffled feathers standing on end.

You should bristle like those cylindrical brushes they use to
    scrub out bottles,
Not even to reach the kindly earth with the soles of your
    prickled feet,
And I would stand by and watch you wriggle and writhe,
    gurgling through the barbs in your throttle
Like a woolly caterpillar pinned on its back—man, that would
    be sweet.

L. A. MacKay

TRAVELER'S CURSE AFTER MISDIRECTION

May they stumble, stage by stage
On an endless pilgrimage,
Dawn and dusk, mile after mile,
At each and every step, a stile;
At each and every step withal
May they catch their feet and fall;
At each and every fall they take
May a bone within them break;
And may the bone that breaks within
Not be, for variation's sake,
Now rib, now thigh, now arm, now shin,
But always, without fail, THE NECK.

Robert Graves
from the Welsh

SKIN THE GOAT'S CURSE ON CAREY*

Before I set sail, I will not fail
    To give that lad my blessing,
And if I had him here there's not much fear
    But he'd get a good top dressing;
By the hat on my head but he'd lie on his bed
    Till the end of next September,
I'd give him good cause to rub his jaws
    And Skin the Goat remember.

But as I won't get the chance to make Carey dance,
    I'll give him my benedictions,
So from my heart's core may he evermore
    Know nothing but afflictions,

May every buck flea from here to Bray
    Jump through the bed that he lies on,
And by some mistake may he shortly take
    A flowing pint of poison.

May his toes fill with corns like a puckawn's¹ horns
    Till he can neither wear slippers or shoes,
With a horrid toothache may he roar like a drake
    And jump like a mad kangaroo.
May a horrid big rat make a hole in his hat
    And chew all the hair off his head,
May the skin of a pig be made into a wig
    And stuck on him when he is dead.

May the devil appear and fill him with fear,
    And give him a kick of his club,
May hard paving stones, and old horses' bones
    Be all that he can get for grub.
May the sun never shine, nor the weather be fine
    Whenever he walks abroad,
Till the day of his death may he have a bad breath
    That will stick like a rotten old cold.

May his old wife be jealous and pitch up the bellows,
    And measure him over the head,
May he get the devil's fright, that will turn him left and right,
    Every night till it knocks him stone dead,
May a horrid baboon jump out of the moon
    And tear his old carcase asunder,
And the day he'll sail, may snow and hail
    Accompany rain and thunder.

That the world may know that Ireland's foe
    Has left the shamrock shore,

And gone to stay at Hudson's Bay,
  Or else in Baltimore.
When I die, my old ghost will sit on his bed-post
  All the night till the cock does crow,
And you may surely swear, while I am there,
  I'll squeeze him before I go.

When the equator is crossed, may the rudder be lost,
  And his vessel be wafted ashore,
To some cannibal isle near the banks of the Nile,
  Where savages jump and roar;
With a big sharp knife may they take his life,
  While his vessel is still afloat,
And pick his bones as clean as stones,
  Is the prayer of poor Skin the Goat.

Anonymous
Irish broadside ballad, 1883

1. *puckawn:* goat.

NELL FLAHERTY'S DRAKE

My name it is Nell, quite candid I tell,
And I lived near Cootehill, I will never deny.
I had a large drake, the truth for to speak,
That my grandmother left me and she goin' to die.
He was wholesome and sound and he weighed twenty pound,
And the universe round I would rove for his sake.
Bad cess to the robber, both drunken and sober,
That murdered Nell Flaherty's beautiful drake!

His neck it was green and most rare to be seen,
He was fit for a queen of the highest degree,

His body was white that would you delight,
He was plump, fat, and heavy, and brisk as a bee,
The dear little fellow his legs they were yellow,
He'd fly like a swallow or dive like a hake;
But some wicked savage to grease his white cabbage
Has murdered Nell Flaherty's beautiful drake.

May his pig never grunt, may his cat never hunt,
That a ghost may him haunt in the dead of the night,
May his hen never lay, may his ass never bray,
May his goat fly away like an old paper kite.
That the flies and the fleas may the wretch ever tease,
And a bitter north breeze make him tremble and shake.
May a four-year-old bug make a nest in the lug
Of the monster that murdered Nell Flaherty's drake.

May his pipe never smoke, and his tea-pot be broke,
And to add to the joke may his kettle ne'er boil,
May he ne'er rest in bed till the hour he is dead,
May he always be fed on lobscouse and fish oil,
May he swell with the gout till his grinders fall out,
May he roar, bawl, and shout with a horrid toothache,
May his temples wear horns and all his toes corns,
The monster that murdered Nell Flaherty's drake.

May his spade never dig, may his sow never pig,
May each nit in his wig be as large as a snail,
May his door have no latch, may his house have no thatch,
May his turkey not hatch, may the rats eat his kale,
May every old fairy from Cork to Dunleary,
Dip him snug and airy in some pond or lake,
Where the eel and the trout may dine on the snout
Of the monster that murdered Nell Flaherty's drake.

May his dog yelp and growl with hunger and cold,

May his wife always scold till his brain goes astray,
May the curse of each hag who e'er carried a bag,
Light on the wag till his beard turns grey;
May monkeys still bite him and mad apes still fight him,
And everyone slight him asleep and awake,
May weasels still gnaw him and jackdaws still claw him,
The monster that murdered Nell Flaherty's drake.

The only good news that I have to diffuse,
Is that long Peter Hughes, and blind piper McPeak,
That big-nosed Bob Manson and buck-toothed Bob Hanson,
Each man has a grandson of my darling drake,
My bird he had dozens of nephews and cousins
And one I must get or my poor heart would break,
To keep my mind easy or else I'll go crazy,
There ends the whole tale of Nell Flaherty's drake.

Anonymous
Irish broadside ballad, nineteenth century

A GLASS OF BEER*

The lanky hank of a she in the inn over there
Nearly killed me for asking the loan of a glass of beer;
May the devil grip the whey-faced slut by the hair,
And beat bad manners out of her skin for a year.

That parboiled ape, with the toughest jaw you will see
On virtue's path, and a voice that would rasp the dead,
Came roaring and raging the minute she looked at me,
And threw me out of the house on the back of my head!

If I asked her master he'd give me a cask a day;
But she, with the beer at hand, not a gill would arrange!

May she marry a ghost and bear him a kitten, and may
The High King of Glory permit her to get the mange.

James Stephens

GAS FROM A BURNER*

Ladies and gents, you are here assembled
To hear why earth and heaven trembled
Because of the black and sinister arts
Of an Irish writer in foreign parts.
He sent me a book ten years ago:
I read it a hundred times or so,
Backwards and forwards, down and up,
Through both the ends of a telescope.
I printed it all to the very last word
But by the mercy of the Lord
The darkness of my mind was rent
And I saw the writer's foul intent.
But I owe a duty to Ireland:
I hold her honour in my hand,
This lovely land that always sent
Her writers and artists to banishment
And in a spirit of Irish fun
Betrayed her own leaders, one by one.
'Twas Irish humour, wet and dry,
Flung quicklime into Parnell's eye;
'Tis Irish brains that save from doom
The leaky barge of the Bishop of Rome
For everyone knows the Pope can't belch
Without the consent of Billy Walsh.
O Ireland my first and only love
Where Christ and Caesar are hand and glove!
O lovely land where the shamrock grows!
(Allow me, ladies, to blow my nose)
To show you for strictures I don't care a button

I printed the poems of Mountainy Mutton
And a play he wrote (you've read it, I'm sure)
Where they talk of *"bastard," "bugger"* and *"whore,"*
And a play on the Word and Holy Paul
And some woman's legs that I can't recall,
Written by Moore, a genuine gent
That lives on his property's ten per cent:
I printed mystical books in dozens:
I printed the table-book of Cousins
Though (asking your pardon) as for the verse
'Twould give you a heartburn on your arse:
I printed folklore from North and South
By Gregory of the Golden Mouth:
I printed poets, sad, silly and solemn:
I printed Patrick What-do-you-Colm:
I printed the great John Milicent Synge
Who soars above on an angel's wing
In the playboy shift that he pinched as swag
From Maunsel's manager's travelling bag.
But I draw the line at that bloody fellow
That was over here dressed in Austrian yellow,
Spouting Italian by the hour
To O'Leary Curtis and John Wyse Power
And writing of Dublin, dirty and dear,
In a manner no blackamoor printer could bear.
Shite and onions! Do you think I'll print
The name of the Wellington Monument,
Sydney Parade and Sandymount tram,
Downes's cakeshop and Williams's jam?
I'm damned if I do—I'm damned to blazes!
Talk about *Irish Names of Places!*
It's a wonder to me, upon my soul,
He forgot to mention Curly's Hole.
No, ladies, my press shall have no share in
So gross a libel on Stepmother Erin.

I pity the poor—that's why I took
A red-headed Scotchman to keep my book.
Poor sister Scotland! Her doom is fell;
She cannot find any more Stuarts to sell.
My conscience is fine as Chinese silk:
My heart is as soft as buttermilk.
Colm can tell you I made a rebate
Of one hundred pounds on the estimate
I gave him for his *Irish Review.*
I love my country—by herrings I do!
I wish you could see what tears I weep
When I think of the emigrant train and ship.
That's why I publish far and wide
My quite illegible railway guide.
In the porch of my printing institute
The poor and deserving prostitute
Plays every night at catch-as-catch-can
With her tight-breeched British artilleryman
And the foreigner learns the gift of the gab
From the drunken draggletail Dublin drab.
Who was it said: Resist not evil?
I'll burn that book, so help me devil.
I'll sing a psalm as I watch it burn
And the ashes I'll keep in a one-handled urn.
I'll penance do with farts and groans
Kneeling upon my marrowbones.
This very next lent I will unbare
My penitent buttocks to the air
And sobbing beside my printing press
My awful sin I will confess.
My Irish foreman from Bannockburn
Shall dip his right hand in the urn
And sign crisscross with reverent thumb
Memento homo upon my bum.

James Joyce

THE BUZZ PLANE

May my Irish grandfather from Tyrells Pass
Grant me the grace to make a proper curse on you, accursed!
You who on a holy Sabbath or a fair holiday
Buzz and circle above my head like the progeny
Of the miscegenation of a buzzard and a bumble-bee.

The great bombers I hate with a lofty hatred,
But you, Harpy, with your unspeakable clatter,
Your sputtering, stuttering, and you know what,
Queering both my music and my silence,
I despise as the perfection of pure nuisance.

Where is the wind-wailed island of mist and seagulls,
Where is the mountain crag mounting to eagles,
Where is the saint's cell, the hermit's citadel,
The nine bean rows and the hive for the honey bee,
Safe from your snoopings, swoopings, and defilements?

May your wife be a gad, a goad, and a gadfly.
May all your bawling, brawling brats never leave you peace.
May you grow bald and birds defile your head.
May your flights be tailspins and your landings crashes.
Fie, fie, fie on you! And the word has power!

Robert Francis

UPTOWN

Yellow Budweiser signs over oaken bars,
"I've seen everything"—the bartender giving me change of $10,
I stared at him amiably eyes thru an obvious Adamic beard—
with Montana musicians homeless in New York, teen age

curly hair themselves—we sat at the antique booth & gossiped,
Madame Grady's literary salon a curious value in New York—
"If I had my way I'd cut off your hair and send you to
       Vietnam"—
"Bless you then" I replied to a hatted thin citizen hurrying to the
       barroom door
upon wet dark Amsterdam Avenue decades later—
"And if I couldn't do that I'd cut your throat" he snarled farewell,
and "Bless you sir" I added as he went to his fate in the rain,—
       dapper Irishman.

Allen Ginsberg

A CURSE AGAINST THE OWNER

Lord Cockroach, Old Sir Empty Belly,
Bring this bad man down.
May his woman's womb ripen
With children blessed
With testicles for ears
And breasts behind their knees.
May he have more than he bargained for.

Barton Sutter

'MINE ENEMY IS GROWING OLD'

Mine Enemy is growing old—
I have at last Revenge—
The Palate of the Hate departs—
If any would avenge

Let him be quick–the Viand flits–
It is a faded Meat–
Anger as soon as fed is dead–
'Tis starving makes it fat–

Emily Dickinson

THE ENEMY'S PORTRAIT

He saw the portrait of his enemy, offered
At auction in a street he journeyed nigh,
That enemy, now late dead, who in his lifetime
Had injured deeply him the passer-by.
"To get that picture, pleased be God, I'll try,
And utterly destroy it; and no more
Shall be inflicted on man's mortal eye
A countenance so sinister and sore!"

And so he bought the painting.   Driving homeward,
"The frame will come in useful," he declared,
"The rest is fuel." On his arrival, weary,
Asked what he bore with him, and how he fared,
He said he had bid for a picture, though he cared
For the frame only: on the morrow he
Would burn the canvas, which could well be spared,
Seeing that it portrayed his enemy.

Next day some other duty found him busy:
The foe was laid his face against the wall;
But on the next he set himself to loosen
The straining-strips.   And then a casual call
Prevented his proceeding therewithal;
And thus the picture waited, day by day,

Its owner's pleasure, like a wretched thrall,
Until a month and more had slipped away.

And then upon a morn he found it shifted,
Hung in a corner by a servitor.
"Why did you take on you to hang that picture?
You know it was the frame I bought it for."
"It stood in the way of every visitor,
And I just hitched it there."—"Well, it must go:
I don't commemorate men whom I abhor.
Remind me 'tis to do.   The frame I'll stow."

But things become forgotten. In the shadow
Of the dark corner hung it by its string,
And there it stayed—once noticed by its owner,
Who said, "Ah me—I must destroy that thing!"
But when he died, there, none remembering,
It hung, till moved to prominence, as one sees;
And comers pause and say, examining,
"I thought they were the bitterest enemies?"

Thomas Hardy

A TEEN-AGER

The high-priced jeans, the new car—she got what
She wanted; she'd been taught to want a lot.
To her girl friend in back, she talked about
Which of her friends shacked up with which. I thought,
"That must be for my benefit. No doubt
She's younger than my daughter. Still, why not?
A glorious redhead. One helps ladies out."

Taking a cigarette, she had to switch
Hands on the wheel to pick a kitchen match
Out of her dungaree shirtpocket which
Seemed quite well filled. Then she reached down to scratch
Fire off those tiny steel teeth that meet, match
And catch closed where her trouserfly's dark patch
Curves under, brightly glittering in her crotch.

I'd seen truck drivers do that. The flames caught:
She lit and sucked in smoke. That's when I got
Snatched back down to facts; I knew why not.
She'd been so spoiled, groomed, fairy-story rich,
She thought hard talk and hard times could be bought
Like poor people's clothes to disguise your niche
In life. Why add my barrel to her notch?

W. D. Snodgrass

TO A LOUDMOUTH PONTIFICATOR

Descend from that pneumatic pedestal,
Thou pompous pestiferous poop!
Avast, thou bellowing burp!
Thy primping, puling, and amorphous bull
Now limply dessicates with sorry stench.
Come down, sirrah,
Ere I do thrum thee such a thwacking thump
As all the bawds of tizzy never twanged.

Ray Mizer

'A PERIPHRASTIC INSULT, NOT A BANAL'

A periphrastic insult, not a banal:
You are not a loud-mouthed and half-assed worm;
You are, sir, magni-oral, semi-anal,
A model for a prophylactic firm.

J. V. Cunningham

TALKING UNION: 1964

The liberator of the laboring
Classes is interviewed on "Meet the Press."
The ruffian who led the Frontenac
Sit-down is missing; his aged surrogate
Is a stout statesman, silver-polled and -tongued,
And silver-tied over a white-on-white
Dress shirt under a trig, if Portly, suit
Tailored by Weatherill. His priestly, bluff
Face with its large pores dryly swallows up
All pointed questions; his brown coin-purse mouth
Doles out small change wrapped in the florid scrip
Of Federalese: "parameters," "key gains,"
"Judgmentally," "negated," "targeting,"
"So, gentlemen, you see." So gentlemen
Are made, not born, with infinite labor pains.

L. E. Sissman

CURSE

Son of a Scots manse though you were
I've taken the rare scunner against you,
You who thieve the golden hours of bairns,
You who bitch up the world's peoples

With crystal images, pitch-black lies,
You who have ended civilised conversation
And dished out licences to print banknotes,
May your soul shrink to the size of a midge
And never rest in a couthie kirkyard
But dart across a million wee screens
And be harassed by TV jingles for ever and ever,
For thine's the kingdom of the *televisor*,
You goddam bloody genius, John Logie Baird!

Robert Greacen

UGLY CHILE

Aw
You so ugly,
You so ugly,
You some ugly chile.
Now the clothes that you wear are not in style;
You look like an ape every time you smile.
Oh how I hate you
You alligator bait you
The homeliest thing I ever saw.
You knock-kneed, pigeon-toed, box-ankled too,
There's a curse on your family and a spell on you.
Your hair is nappy.
Who's your pappy?
You some ugly chile.

You five by five and double-jointed too.
There's a curse on your family and it fell on you.
Your teeth are yella, who's your fella?
You some ugly chile.

Clarence Williams
American popular song, 1917

SOLILOQUY OF THE SPANISH CLOISTER

Gr-r-r—there go, my heart's abhorrence!
  Water your damned flower-pots, do!
If hate killed men, Brother Lawrence,
  God's blood, would not mine kill you!
What? your myrtle-bush wants trimming?
  Oh, that rose has prior claims—
Needs its leaden vase filled brimming?
  Hell dry you up with its flames!

At the meal we sit together;
  Salve tibi! I must hear
Wise talk of the kind of weather,
  Sort of season, time of year:
Not a plenteous cork-crop: scarcely
  Dare we hope oak-galls, I doubt;
What's the Latin name for "parsley"?
  What's the Greek name for "swine's snout"?

Whew! We'll have our platter burnished,
  Laid with care on our own shelf!
With a fire-new spoon we're furnished,
  And a goblet for ourself,
Rinsed like something sacrificial
  Ere 'tis fit to touch our chaps—
Marked with L. for our initial!
  (He-he! There his lily snaps!)

Saint, forsooth! While brown Dolores
  Squats outside the Convent bank
With Sanchicha, telling stories,
  Steeping tresses in the tank,
Blue-black, lustrous, thick like horsehairs,

—Can't I see his dead eye glow,
Bright as 'twere a Barbary corsair's?
(That is, if he'd let it show!)

When he finishes refection,
   Knife and fork he never lays
Cross-wise, to my recollection,
   As do I, in Jesu's praise.
I, the Trinity illustrate,
   Drinking watered orange-pulp—
In three sips the Arian frustrate;
   While he drains his at one gulp!

Oh, those melons! if he's able
   We're to have a feast; so nice!
One goes to the Abbot's table,
   All of us get each a slice.
How go on your flowers? None double?
   Not one fruit-sort can you spy?
Strange!—And I, too, at such trouble,
   Keep them close-nipped on the sly!

There's a great text in Galatians,
   Once you trip on it, entails
Twenty-nine distinct damnations,
   One sure, if another fails;
If I trip him just a-dying,
   Sure of heaven as sure can be,
Spin him round and send him flying
   Off to hell, a Manichee?

Or, my scrofulous French novel
   On grey paper with blunt type!
Simply glance at it, you grovel

Hand and foot in Belail's gripe;
If I double down its pages
At the woeful sixteenth print,
When he gathers his greengages,
Ope a sieve and slip it in't?

Or, there's Satan!—one might venture
Pledge one's soul to him, yet leave
Such a flaw in the indenture
As he'd miss till, past retrieve,
Blasted lay that rose-acacia
We're so proud of! *Hy, Zy, Hine.* . . .
'St, there's Vespers! *Plena gratia*
Ave, Virgo! Gr-r-r—you swine!

Robert Browning

'BURY HIM DEEP'

Bury him deep. So damned a work should lie
Nearer the Devil than man. Make him a bed
Beneath some lock-jawed hell, that never yawns
With earthquake or eruption; and so deep
That he may hear the devil and his wife
In bed, talking secrets.

Thomas Lovell Beddoes

'I MUSE NOT'

I muse not that your dog turds oft doth eat:
To a tongue that licks your lips, a turd's sweet meat.

Francis Davison

FOR A FRIEND

Your blood reappears on my hands.
When you murdered the real man
Years ago, hacking his bones
Under moss and tree roots,
I kept hoping they would sprout
Into giants. One October day
You were impossible.
I decided to take your brilliant
And hateful love,
Tattooing it into my pigment.

You have made it all disposable;
False teeth, sixty years, a furrowed,
Tendinous will. The power shovel
Collects pieces of an old man. Smoke
Rises red and sticky as tomato
Dust. I wash my hands, and calcium
Cysts tick through my fingerjoints.

David Steingass

IF JUSTICE MOVED*

Dante had the right idea,
consigning traitors
to the deepest pits of Hell—

you, traitor with beard scarcely
formed, belong in ice confined
or gnashed by Satan's bloody teeth.

The master poet limned no woman
more betrayed than Dido was—

no lines depict a bitter face like mine . . .

You mowed my grass, spread sandwiches
at my kitchen table. Nights,
you smudged tears with dirty knuckles.

I trusted you to tend my child
and you have left her bleeding,
limp as the stuffed tiger

empty-eyed in his jungle.
If I understood, I could forgive—
but, seeing her, I'd give my chance

at Heaven to take up Ugolino's place.
If Ruggiero's neck be yours—
I'd gnaw on it a thousand years.

Bettie M. Sellers

INCANTATION TO GET RID OF A SOMETIME FRIEND

Peel off me
like last year's
snake skin

Fall off me
like a weakened
thumbtack

Dry up
like
unwatered
weed

Emanuel diPasquale

WINTER SAINT

In the summer I live so
close to my neighbor I
can hear him sweat:

all my forced bushes, leafy
and birdy, do not
prevent this:

his drawers wrenched
off his sticky butt
clutch my speech white:

his beery mouth wakes up
under my tongue: his
lawnmower wilts my cereal:

I do not like to hear him
wheeze over difficult weeds:
I don't like his squishy toes:

I'm for ice and shutters
and the miles and miles
winter clears between us.

A. R. Ammons

BEYOND WORDS

That row of icicles along the gutter
Feels like my armory of hate;
And you, you . . . you, you utter . . .
You wait!

Robert Frost

V.

COLLECTIVE
DETESTATIONS

Sure England hath the hemeroids, and these
On the North postern of the patient seize,
Like leeches: thus they physically thirst
After our blood, but in the cure shall burst.
JOHN CLEVELAND, "The Rebel Scot"

This indigested vomit of the sea
Fell to the Dutch by just propriety.
ANDREW MARVELL, "The Character of Holland"

Italians hate Yugoslavs,
South Africans hate the Dutch
And I don't like anybody very much.
SHELDON HARNICK, "The Merry Little Minuet,"
American popular song, 1953

In the nightmare of the dark
All the dogs of Europe bark,
And the living nations wait,
Each sequestered in its hate . . .
W. H. AUDEN, "In Memory of W. B. Yeats"

THE BLACKSMITHS*

Sooty, swart smiths,
> smattered with smoke,
Drive me to death
> with the din of their dents.
Such noise at night
> no man heard, never:
With knavish cries
> and clattering of knocks!
The crooked cretins
> call out, "Coal, coal!"
And blow their bellows,
> that all their brains burst:
"Huff, puff!" says that one;
> "haff, paff!" that other.
They spit and sprawl
> and spill many spells;
They gnaw and gnash,
> they groan together
And hold their heat
> with their hard hammers.
Of bullhide are their
> broad aprons made;
Their shanks be shackled
> for the fiery flinders;
Heavy hammers they have
> that are hard-handled,
Stark strokes they strike
> on a steely stump:
LUS, BUS! LAS, DAS!
> rants the row—
So doleful a dream,
> the Devil destroy it!

The master lengthens little
                    and labors less,
Twines a two
            and touches a trey:
Tick, tack! hick, hack!
                    ticket, tacket! tyke, take!
LUS, BUS! LAS, DAS!
                    Such lives they lead,
These cobblemares:
                    Christ give them grief!
May none of these waterburners
                    by night have his rest!

                                Anonymous
                        English, fifteenth century
                    modern rendering by Wesli Court

[AN EXECRATION AGAINST WHORES]*

Shall I expound "whore" to you? sure, I shall;
I'll give their perfect character. They are, first,
Sweetmeats which rot the eater; in man's nostril,
Poisoned perfumes; they're cozening alchemy;
Shipwracks in calmest weather! What are whores?
Cold Russian winters, that appear so barren
As if that Nature had forgot the spring;
They are the true material fire of Hell,
Worse than those tributes i'the Low Countries paid,
Exactions upon meat, drink, garments, sleep,
Ay, even on man's perdition, his sin;
They are those brittle evidences of law
Which forfeit all a wretched man's estate
For leaving out one syllable. What are whores?

They are those flattering bells have all one tune
At weddings and at funerals. Your rich whores
Are only treasuries by extortion filled
And emptied by curst riot. They are worse,
Worse than dead bodies which are begged at gallows
And wrought upon by surgeons, to teach man
Wherein he is imperfect. What's a whore?
She's like the guilty counterfeited coin
Which, whosoe'er first stamps it, brings in trouble
All that receive it.

John Webster
The White Devil, III, ii

SONNET 18*

Avenge O Lord thy slaughtered saints, whose bones
 Lie scattered on the Alpine mountains cold,
 Ev'n them who kept thy truth so pure of old
When all our fathers worshipped stocks and stones,
Forget not: in Thy book record their groans
 Who were thy sheep and in their ancient fold
 Slain by the bloody Piemontese that rolled
Mother with infant down the rocks. Their moans
The vales redoubled to the hills, and they
 To Heav'n. Their martyred blood and ashes sow
O'er all th'Italian fields where still doth sway
 The triple tyrant: that from these may grow
A hundredfold, who having learnt thy way
 Early may fly the Babylonian woe.

John Milton

HOW BEASTLY THE BOURGEOIS IS—

How beastly the bourgeois is
especially the male of the species—

Presentable eminently presentable—
shall I make you a present of him?

Isn't he handsome? isn't he healthy? Isn't he a fine specimen?
doesn't he look the fresh clean englishman, outside?
Isn't it god's own image? tramping his thirty miles a day
after partridges, or a little rubber ball?
wouldn't you like to be like that, well off, and quite the thing?

Oh, but wait!
Let him meet a new emotion, let him be faced with another man's
    need,
let him come home to a bit of moral difficulty, let life face
    him with a new demand on his understanding
and then watch him go soggy, like a wet meringue.
Watch him turn into a mess, either a fool or a bully.
Just watch the display of him, confronted with a new
    demand on his intelligence,
a new life-demand.

How beastly the bourgeois is
especially the male of the species—

Nicely groomed, like a mushroom
standing there so sleek and erect and eyeable—
and like a fungus, living on the remains of bygone life
sucking his life out of the dead leaves of greater life than his own.

And even so, he's stale, he's been there too long.
Touch him, and you'll find he's all gone inside

just like an old mushroom, all wormy inside, and hollow
under a smooth skin and an upright appearance.

Full of seething, wormy, hollow feelings
rather nasty—
How beastly the bourgeois is!

Standing in their thousands, these appearances, in damp
    England
what a pity they can't all be kicked over
like sickening toadstools, and left to melt back, swiftly
into the soil of England.

D. H. Lawrence

DOCKER

There, in the corner, staring at his drink.
The cap juts like a gantry's crossbeam,
Cowling plated forehead and sledgehead jaw.
Speech is clamped in the lips' vice.

That fist would drop a hammer on a Catholic—
Oh yes, that kind of thing could start again;
The only Roman collar he tolerates
Smiles all round his sleek pint of porter.

Mosaic imperatives bang home like rivets;
God is a foreman with certain definite views
Who orders life in shifts of work and leisure.
A factory horn will blare the Resurrection.

He sits, strong and blunt as a Celtic cross,
Clearly used to silence and an armchair:
Tonight the wife and children will be quiet
At slammed door and smoker's cough in the hall.

Seamus Heaney

[A CURSE ON MINE-OWNERS]

May God above
Send down a dove
With wings as sharp as razors
To cut the throats
Of those old bloats
Who cut poor miners' wages!

Anonymous
American folk verse, Pennsylvania, ca. 1900

A CURSE

If I forget thee not, New York,
May my ulcer of exile fork

Your sons, may impetigo and the yaws
Be on sale in all the stores;

May you like Chicagoans pronounce your r's,
May the handles fall from your doors

If I forget thee not; may your zippers stick
And drains plug, may you always eat at Nedicks;

May adultery be your only sweet,
No stain ever wash from a sheet;

May the theatres play one movie forever,
May the telephone ring never;

May the laundries take the buttons from your shirts
And the elastic rot on your skirts

If I forget thee not; may your letters be unsent,
May your Sunday dinners never end;

May the corks fall into the wine
And your fish be all scale or all spine;

May oil be found in Central Park,
May there be no place for cars to park;

May the ocean run from your taps
And Jersey claim you on all the maps;

May slugs jam every turnstile slot
If I forget thee not.

Irving Feldman

COLOGNE

In Köhln, a town of monks and bones,
And pavements fang'd with murderous stones
And rags, and hags, and hideous wenches;
I counted two and seventy stenches,
All well defined, and several stinks!
Ye Nymphs that reign o'er sewers and sinks,
The river Rhine, it is well known,
Doth wash your city of Cologne;
But tell me, Nymphs, what power divine
Shall henceforth wash the river Rhine?

Samuel Taylor Coleridge

ON MY JOYFUL DEPARTURE FROM THE CITY OF COLOGNE

As I am a Rhymer
And now at least a merry one,
Mr. Mum's Rudesheimer
And the church of St. Geryon
Are the two things alone
That deserve to be known
In the body-and-soul-stinking town of Cologne.

Samuel Taylor Coleridge

THE FOX-HUNTERS

What Gods are these? Bright red, or white and green,
Some of them jockey-capp'd and some in hats,
The gods of vermin have their runs, like rats.
Each has six legs, four moving, pendent two,
Like bottled tails, the tilting four between.
Behold Land-Interest's compound Man-and-Horse,
Which so enchants his outraged helot-crew,
Hedge-gapping, with his horn, and view-halloo,
O'er hunter's clover—glorious broom and gorse!
The only crop his godship ever grew:
Except his crop of hate, and smouldering ire,
And cloak'd contempt, of coward insult born,
And hard-faced labour, paid with straw for corn,
And fain to reap it with a scythe of fire.

Ebenezer Elliott

IN RESPONSE TO A RUMOR THAT THE OLDEST WHOREHOUSE IN WHEELING, WEST VIRGINIA, HAS BEEN CONDEMNED

I will grieve alone,
As I strolled alone, years ago, down along
The Ohio shore.
I hid in the hobo jungle weeds
Upstream from the sewer main,
Pondering, gazing.

I saw, down river,
At Twenty-third and Water Streets
By the vinegar works,
The doors open in early evening.
Swinging their purses, the women
Poured down the long street to the river
And into the river.

I do not know how it was
They could drown every evening.
What time near dawn did they climb up the other shore,
Drying their wings?

For the river at Wheeling, West Virginia,
Has only two shores:
The one in hell, the other
In Bridgeport, Ohio.

And nobody would commit suicide, only
To find beyond death
Bridgeport, Ohio.

James Wright

THE INVENTION OF NEW JERSEY

Place a custard stand in a garden
or in place of a custard stand
    place a tumbled-down custard stand
in place of a tumbled-down custard stand
    place miniature golf in a garden
    and an advertisement for miniature golf
        shaped for no apparent reason
        like an old Dutch windmill
in place of a swamp
    place a swamp

          or a pizzeria called the Tower of Pizza
          sporting a scale model
             of the Tower of Pisa
          or a water tower resembling
             a roll-on deodorant
          or a Dixie Cup factory
             with a giant metal Dixie Cup on the roof

In place of wolverines, rabbits, or melons
    place a vulcanizing plant
in place of a deer
    place an iron deer
    at a lawn furniture store
    selling iron deer
        Negro jockeys
        Bavarian gnomes
        and imitation grottoes
        with electric Infants of Prague
in place of phosphorescence
    of marshy ground at night
        place smears of rubbish fires

in place of brown water with minnows
    place brown water
                gigantic landlords
                in the doorways of apartment houses
                which look like auto showrooms
                auto showrooms which look like diners
                diners which look like motels
                motels which look like plastic chair
                                  covers
                plastic chair covers which look like
                plastic table covers which look like
                              plastic bags
                the mad scientist of Secaucus
                invents a plastic cover
                to cover the lawn
                with millions of perforations
                for the grass to poke through

In place of the straight lines of grasses
    place the straight lines of gantries
in place of lights in the window
    place lighted refineries
in place of a river
    place the road like a slim pair of pants
        set to dry beside a neon frankfurter
in place of New Jersey
    place a plastic New Jersey

                on weekends a guy has nothing to do
                except drive around in a convertible
                counting the shoe stores
                and thinking of screwing
                    his date beside him
                    a faintly bilious look
                    perpetually on her face

                                    Jack Anderson

THE CALIFORNIANS

Beautiful and blond they come, the Californians,
Holding their blond beautiful children by the hand;
They come with healthy sunlight in tall hair;
Smiling and empty they stride back over the land.

Tanned and tempting, they reverse the pioneer
And glide back to Atlantic shores from their state,
And shows on Broadway have tall, oh, very tall girls,
To replace the shorter kind we generate.

California men put airplanes on like shoes
To swoop through the air they beautifully advertise,
And the women of California are splendid women,
With nothing, nothing, nothing behind their eyes.

Oranges, movies, smiles, and rainless weather,
Delightful California, you spread to our view,
And the whitest teeth, the brownest, most strokable shoulders,
And a hateful wish to be empty and tall like you.

Theodore Spencer

GOOD OLD REBEL

Oh, I'm a good old rebel, that's what I am,
And for this land of freedom, I don't give a damn;
I'm glad I fought agin her, I only wish we'd won,
And I ain't axed any pardon for anything I've done.

I fought with old Bob Lee for three years about,
Got wounded in four places and starved at Point Lookout.
I caught the rheumatism a-campin' in the snow,
But I killed a chance of Yankees and I wish I'd killed some mo'!

Three hundred thousand Yankees is dead in Southern dust,
We got three hundred thousand before they conquered us;
They died of Southern fever, of Southern steel and shot—
I wish they was three million instead of what we got.

I hate the Constitution, this great republic, too;
I hate the nasty eagle, and the uniform so blue;
I hate their glorious banner, and all their flags and fuss.
Those lying, thieving Yankees, I hate 'em wuss and wuss.

I hate the Yankee nation and everything they do;
I hate the Declaration of Independence, too;
I hate the glorious Union, 'tis dripping with our blood;
I hate the striped banner, I fought it all I could.

I won't be reconstructed! I'm better now than them;
And for a carpetbagger, I don't give a damn;
So I'm off for the frontier, soon as I can go,
I'll prepare me a weapon and start for Mexico.

I can't take up my musket and fight them now no mo',
But I'm not goin' to love 'em and that is certain sho';
And I don't want no pardon for what I was or am,
I won't be reconstructed and I don't give a damn.

Innes Randolph
American popular song, ca. 1870

'HATE AND DEBATE ROME
THROUGH THE WORLD HATH SPREAD'

Hate and debate Rome through the world hath spread,
Yet Roma *amor* is, if backward read.
Then is't not strange Rome hate should foster?   No:
For out of backward love all hate doth grow.

Sir John Harington

ON A RHINE STEAMER

Republic of the West,
    Enlightened, free, sublime,
Unquestionably best
    Production of our time.

The telephone is thine,
    And thine the Pullman car,
The caucus, the divine
    Intense electric star.

To thee we likewise owe
    The venerable names
Of Edgar Allan Poe
    And Mr. Henry James.

In short, it's due to thee,
    Thou kind of Western star,
That we have come to be
    Precisely what we are.

But every now and then,
    It cannot be denied,

You breed a kind of men
Who are not dignified,

Or courteous or refined,
Benevolent or wise,
Or gifted with a mind
Beyond the common size,

Or notable for tact,
Agreeable to me,
Or anything, in fact,
That people ought to be.

James Kenneth Stephen

CHRISTIANS AT WAR*

(Tune: "Onward, Christian Soldiers")

Onward, Christian soldiers! Duty's way is plain;
Slay your Christian neighbors, or by them be slain.
Pulpiteers are spouting effervescent swill,
God above is calling you to rob and rape and kill,
All your acts are sanctified by the Lamb on high;
If you love the Holy Ghost, go murder, pray and die.

Onward, Christian soldiers, rip and tear and smite!
Let the gentle Jesus bless your dynamite.
Splinter skulls with shrapnel, fertilize the sod;
Folks who do not speak your tongue deserve the curse of God.
Smash the doors of every home, pretty maidens seize;
Use your might and sacred right to treat them as you please.

Onward, Christian soldiers! Eat and drink your fill;
Rob with bloody fingers, Christ O.K.'s the bill.

Steal the farmers' savings, take their grain and meat;
Even though the children starve, the Savior's bums must eat.
Burn the peasants' cottages, orphans leave bereft;
In Jehovah's holy name, wreak ruin right and left.

Onward, Christian soldiers! Drench the land with gore;
Mercy is a weakness all the gods abhor.
Bayonet the babies, jab the mothers, too;
Hoist the cross of Calvary to hallow all you do.
File your bullets' noses flat, poison every well;
God decrees your enemies must all go plumb to hell.

Onward, Christian soldiers! Blighting all you meet,
Trampling human freedom under pious feet.
Praise the Lord whose dollar sign dupes his favored race!
Make the foreign trash respect your bullion brand of grace.
Trust in mock salvation, service as pirates' tools;
History will say of you: "That pack of G . . . d . . . fools."

John F. Kendrick

MALEDICTION

You who dump the beer cans in the lake;
Who in the strict woods sow
The bulbous polyethylene retorts;
Who from your farting car
With spiffy rear-suspension toss
Your tissues, mustard-streaked, upon
The generating moss; who drop
The squamules of your reckless play,
Grease-wrappers, unspare parts, lie-labeled

Cultures even flies would scorn
To spawn on—total Zed, my kinsman
Ass-on-wheels, my blare-bred bray
And burden,
    may the nice crabs thread
Your private wilds with turnpikes; weasels'
Condoms squish between your toes,
And plastic-coated toads squat *plop*
Upon your morning egg—may gars
Come nudge you from your inner-tube,
Perch hiss you to the bottom, junked,
A discard, your dense self your last
Enormity.

Barry Spacks

NINE CHARMS AGAINST THE HUNTER

In the last bar on the way to your wild game,
May the last beer tilt you over among friends
And keep you there till sundown—failing that,
A breakdown on the road, ditching you gently
Where you may hunt for lights and a telephone.
Or may your smell go everywhere through the brush,
Upwind or crosswind. May your feet come down
Invariably crunching loudly on dry sticks.
Or may whatever crosses your hairlines—
The flank of elk or moose, the scut of a deer,
The blurring haunch of a bear, or another hunter
Gaping along his sights at the likes of you—
May they catch you napping or freeze you with buck fever.
Or if you fire, may the stock butting your shoulder
Knock you awake around your bones as you miss,

Or then and there, may the noise pour through your mind
Imaginary deaths to redden your daydreams:
Dazed animals sprawling forward on dead leaves,
Thrashing and kicking, spilling themselves as long
As you could wish, as hard, as game,
And then, if you need it, imaginary skinning,
Plucking of liver and lights, unraveling guts,
Beheading trophies to your heart's content.
Or if these charms have failed and the death is real,
May it fatten you, hour by hour, for the trapped hunter
Whose dull knife beats the inside of your chest.

David Wagoner

WARMING UP FOR THE REAL THING

for the newspaper vendor at Kendall Square;
and my father, and his mother; and others

oh, you foulbreathed destroyer of children and villages,
oh, you scabskinned loose lump of flesh and slack veins,
I want you to die
like this: slowly: in two dozen ways:

if you live in a racist suburb, I hope you turn coat-hanger
    black,
    from newsprint that rubs off the headlines you won't
    let me read
    and when you go home tonight, your neighbors, your
    family
    your very own children, burn you on your front lawn
    (you cross old man) then spit on your ashes

if you live alone, when you go home tonight may your
    lightbulbs
all explode in your face, the fluorescent fixtures
light your lungs green with mercury, give you con-
    vulsions;
or let it happen here by your newspaper stand: buck,
    back on the street:
wet your pants and the sidewalk, roll in it,
(and I hope your gallbladder bursts and your liver
    turns into leather
and your eyeballs pop out of their sockets and spoil
    your vest),
and everyone passing by gets a free look at the head-
    lines,
for as long as they want, and no one gives you a cent,
    and you know it, you know it,
and if you have grandchildren I hope you turn into chocolate,
    a five-foot-six-inch Easter bunny, and they eat you up
until they get sick, and puke you out, and their mouths
have to be washed out with soap, and their stomachs
    pumped,
 and then they never have you to weigh down their lives
    any more,

and I want you to live through this all: be resurrected: feel
    all the pain
over and over, and know why you have it,
until the day you walk by the Necco factory
one time too many, and get acne deep in your lungs,
and die   scratching it
with a coathanger.

Lee Rudolph

A STUDY OF READING HABITS

When getting my nose in a book
Cured most things short of school,
It was worth ruining my eyes
To know I could still keep cool,
And deal out the old right hook
To dirty dogs twice my size.

Later, with inch-thick specs,
Evil was just my lark:
Me and my cloak and fangs
Had ripping times in the dark.
The women I clubbed with sex!
I broke them up like meringues.

Don't read much now: the dude
Who lets the girl down before
The hero arrives, the chap
Who's yellow and keeps the store,
Seem far too familiar. Get stewed:
Books are a load of crap.

Philip Larkin

THE DAUGHTERS OF THE HORSELEECH*

The daughters of the horseleech crying "Give! Give!"
Implore the young men for the blood of martyrs.
How shall we keep the old senator alive
Unless we satisfy his thirst for cultures?

Entreat the rat, the weasel, and the fox

To forage for a toothless master;
Have mercy, boys, on the monkey in his box;
Dear Judas goat, lead out the sheep to slaughter,

For if the warlock with the gilded claws
Withers away, and of his bones are waters,
Who will transmute our foreheads into brass
And who will keep his five charming daughters?

Stanley Kunitz

VI.

NOBLES,
STATESMEN,
PRELATES
&
TOP BRASS

As long as they fear me, let them hate me
as much as they like.
CALIGULA, quoted by Suetonius

'Ruin seize thee, ruthless King!
Confusion on thy banners wait . . .'
THOMAS GRAY, "The Bard: A Pindaric Ode"

Detestation of the high is the involuntary homage of the low.
CHARLES DICKENS, A Tale of Two Cities

I do not hate him nearly as much as I fear I ought to.
THOMAS CARLYLE, of the Bishop of Oxford

HELEN

All Greece hates
the still eyes in the white face,
the lustre as of olives
where she stands,
and the white hands.

All Greece reviles
the wan face when she smiles,
hating it deeper still
when it grows wan and white,
remembering past enchantments
and past ills.

Greece sees, unmoved,
God's daughter, born of love,
the beauty of cool feet
and slenderest knees,
could love indeed the maid,
only if she were laid,
white ash amid funereal cypresses.

H.D.

THE VOWS

When the plate was at pawn and the fob[1] at an ebb
And the spider might weave in our stomach its web,
Our stomach as empty as brain,
Then Charles without acre
Made these vows to his Maker
If ere he saw England again:

I will have a religion then, all of mine own
Where Papist from Protestant shall not be known,
But if it grow troublesome I will have none.

I will have a fine Parliament always to friend
That shall furnish me treasure as fast as I spend,
But when they will not they shall be at an end.

I will have as fine bishops as were e'er made with hands,
With consciences flexible to my commands,
But if they displease me I will have all their lands.

I will have my fine Chancellor bear all the sway,
Yet *if* men should clamour I'll pack him away
And yet call him home again soon as I may.

I will have a fine navy to conquer the seas
And the Dutch shall give caution for their provinces,
But if they should beat me I will do what they please.

I will have a new London instead of the old,
With wide streets and uniform, of mine own mold,
But if they build it too fast, I will soon make them hold.

I will have a fine son (in making though marred),
If not o'er a kingdom to reign, o'er my guard,
And successor, if not to me, to Gerrard.

I will have a fine court, with ne'er an old face,
And always who beards me shall have the next grace,
And I either will vacate or buy him a place.

I will have a Privy Council to sit always still,
I will have a fine junto to do what I will,
I will have two fine secretarys piss through one quill.

I will have a privy-purse without a control,
I will wink all the while my revenue is stole,
And if any be questioned I'll answer the whole.

But whatever it cost I will have a fine whore
As bold as Al'ce Pierce and as fair as Jane Shore,
And when I am weary of her I'll have more.

Of my pimp I will make my *Ministre premier*,
My bawd shall ambassadors send far and near,
And my wench shall dispose of the *congé d'eslire*.[2]

If this please not, I'll reign upon any condition,
Miss and I will both learn to live on exhibition,
And I'll first put the Church then my crown in commission.

I will have a fine tunic, a shash and a vest,
Though not rule like the Turk yet I will be so drest,
And who knows but the mode may soon bring in the rest?

I will have a fine pond and a pretty decoy[3]
Where the ducks and the drakes may their freedoms enjoy
And quack in their language still, *Vive le Roy.*

Andrew Marvell

1. *fob:* purse. 2. *congé d'eslire:* right of making appointments to public office. 3. *decoy:* a gate or baffle made of netting, to prevent waterfowl from escaping.

ON QUEEN CAROLINE'S DEATHBED

Here lies wrapped up in forty thousand towels
The only proof that Caroline had bowels.

Alexander Pope

ENGLAND IN 1819*

An old, mad, blind, despised, and dying king[1]—
Princes, the dregs of their dull race, who flow
Through public scorn—mud from a muddy spring;
Rulers who neither see, nor feel, nor know,
But leechlike to their fainting country cling,
Till they drop, blind in blood, without a blow;
A people starved and stabbed in the untilled field—
An army, which liberticide and prey
Makes as a two-edged sword to all who wield;
Golden and sanguine laws which tempt and slay;
Religion Christless, Godless—a book sealed;
A Senate—Time's worst statute[2] unrepealed—
Are graves, from which a glorious Phantom may
Burst, to illumine our tempestuous day.

Percy Bysshe Shelley

1. *king:* George III. 2. *statute:* the Test Act, curbing Irish rights.

SIMILES FOR TWO POLITICAL CHARACTERS OF 1819*

I

As from an ancestral oak
    Two empty ravens sound their clarion,
Yell by yell, and croak by croak,
When they scent the noonday smoke
    Of fresh human carrion:—

II

As two gibbering night-birds flit
    From their bowers of deadly yew

Through the night to frighten it,
When the moon is in a fit,
    And the stars are none, or few:—

III

As a shark and dog-fish wait
    Under an Atlantic isle
For the Negro-ship, whose freight
Is the theme of their debate,
    Wrinkling their red gills the while—

IV

Are ye, two vultures sick for battle,
    Two scorpions under one wet stone,
Two bloodless wolves whose dry throats rattle,
Two crows perched on the murrained cattle,
    Two vipers tangled into one.

                                        Percy Bysshe Shelley

[GEORGE III]

In the first year of freedom's second dawn
    Died George the Third; although no tyrant, one
Who shielded tyrants, till each sense withdrawn
    Left him nor mental nor external sun:
A better farmer ne'er brushed dew from lawn,
    A worse king never left a realm undone!
He died—but left his subjects still behind,
One, half as mad—and t'other, no less blind.

He died! his death made no great stir on earth:
    His burial made some pomp; there was profusion

Of velvet, gilding, brass, and no great dearth
    Of aught but tears—save those shed by collusion.
For these things may be bought at their truth worth;
    Of elegy there was the due infusion—
Bought also; and the torches, cloaks, and banners,
Heralds, and relics of old Gothic manners,

Formed a sepulchral melodrame. Of all
    The fools who flocked to swell or see the show,
Who cared about the corpse? The funeral
    Made the attraction, and the black the woe,
There throbbed not there a thought which pierced the pall;
    And when the gorgeous coffin was laid low,
It seemed the mockery of Hell to fold
The rottenness of eighty years in gold.

So mix his body with the dust! It might
    Return to what it *must* far sooner, were
The natural compound left alone to fight
    Its way back into earth, and fire, and air;
But the unnatural balsams merely blight
    What nature made him at his birth, as bare
As the mere million's base unmummied clay—
Yet all his spices but prolong decay.

He's dead—and upper earth with him has done;
    He's buried; save the undertaker's bill,
Or lapidary scrawl, the world is gone
    For him, unless he left a German will:
But where's the proctor who will ask his son?
    In whom his qualities are reigning still,
Except that household virtue, most uncommon,
Of constancy to a bad, ugly woman.

George Gordon, Lord Byron
The Vision of Judgment

BUCHLYVIE

Baron of Buchlyvie,
May the foul fiend drive ye,
And a' tae pieces rive ye,
 For buildin' sic a toun,
Where there's neither horse meat nor man's meat,
 Nor a chair to sit doon.

Anonymous
Scottish popular verse

A LITTLE SHRUB GROWING BY

Ask not to know this man. If fame should speak
His name in any metal, it would break.
Two letters were enough the plague to tear
Out of his grave, and poison every ear.
A parcel of Court-dirt, a heap, a mass
Of all vice hurled together, there he was,
Proud, false, and treacherous, vindictive, all
That thought can add, unthankful, the lay-stall
Of putrid flesh alive! of blood, the sink!
And so I leave to stir him, lest he stink.

Ben Jonson

ON LORD HOLLAND'S SEAT NEAR MARGATE, KENT*

Old and abandoned by each venal friend,
 Here H[olland] took the pious resolution
To smuggle some few years and strive to mend
 A broken character and constitution.

On this congenial spot he fixed his choice;
    Earl Godwin trembled for his neighbouring sand;
Here seagulls scream and cormorants rejoice
    And mariners, though shipwrecked, dread to land.
Here reign the blustering North and blighting East,
    No tree is heard to whisper, bird to sing;
Yet Nature cannot furnish out the feast,
    Art he invokes new horrors still to bring.
Now mouldering fanes and battlements arise,
    Arches and turrets nodding to their fall,
Unpeopled palaces delude his eyes,
    And mimic desolation covers all.
"Ah," said the sighing peer, "had Bute been true,
    Nor Shelburne's, Rigby's, Calcraft's friendship vain,
Far other scenes than these had blessed our view
    And realized the ruins that we feign.
Purged by the sword and beautified by fire,
    Then had we seen proud London's hated walls:
Owls might have hooted in St Peter's choir
    And foxes stunk and littered in St Paul's."

Thomas Gray

'HERE LIES SIR TACT'

Here lies Sir Tact, a diplomatic fellow
Whose silence was not golden, but just yellow.

Timothy Steele

THE DUKE IS THE LAD TO FRIGHTEN A LASS

The Duke is the lad to frighten a lass,
    Galloping, dreary duke;
The Duke is the lad to frighten a lass,
He's an ogre to meet, and the devil to pass,
    With his charger prancing,
    Grim eye glancing,
    Chin, like a Mufti,
    Grizzled and tufty,
Galloping, dreary Duke.

Ye misses, beware of the neighborhood
    Of this galloping, dreary Duke;
Avoid him, all who see no good
In being run o'er by a Prince of the Blood.
    For, surely, no nymph is
    Fond of a grim phiz,
    And of the married,
    Whole crowds have miscarried
At sight of this dreary Duke.

Thomas Moore

THE TOAD-EATER

What of earls with whom you have supt,
    And of dukes that you dined with yestreen?
Lord! an insect's an insect at most,
    Though it crawl on the curls of a Queen.

Robert Burns

EPITAPH ON JAMES GRIEVE, LAIRD OF BOGHEAD

Here lies Boghead amang the dead
In hopes to get salvation;
But if such as he in Heaven may be,
Then welcome—hail! damnation.

Robert Burns

GIN THE GOODWIFE STINT

The ploughland has gone to bent
and the pasture to heather;
gin the goodwife stint,
she'll keep the house together.

Gin the goodwife stint
and the bairns hunger
the Duke can get his rent
one year longer.

The Duke can get his rent
and we can get our ticket
twa pund emigrant
on a C.P.R. packet.

Basil Bunting

A MILTONIC SONNET FOR MR. JOHNSON
ON HIS REFUSAL OF PETER HURD'S OFFICIAL PORTRAIT

Heir to the office of a man not dead
Who drew our Declaration up, who planned
Range and Rotunda with his drawing-hand
And harbored Palestrina in his head,
Who would have wept to see small nations dread
The imposition of our cattle-brand,
With public truth at home mistold or banned,
And in whose term no army's blood was shed,

Rightly you say the picture is too large
Which Peter Hurd by your appointment drew,
And justly call that Capitol too bright
Which signifies our people in your charge;
Wait, Sir, and see how time will render you,
Who talk of vision but are weak of sight.

6 January 1967   • *Richard Wilbur*

CAMPAIGN PROMISE

During the Great Debates,[1] he tried a joke
and nothing happened. For an instant, hatred
for everything he saw leapt from his eyes
to his mouth, and down his arm to one hand
the camera caught and held as it gripped something—
the lectern, a table's corner, I forget what—
which, had it been alive, he would have killed.

Henry Taylor

1. *Great Debates:* between John F. Kennedy and Richard M. Nixon on television in 1960.

ON A POLITICIAN

How richly, with ridiculous display,
The Politician's corpse was laid away.
While all of his acquaintance sneered and slanged,
I wept: for I had longed to see him hanged.

Hilaire Belloc

'A POLITICIAN'

a politician is an arse upon
which everyone has sat except a man

E. E. Cummings

'LAST CAME, AND LAST DID GO'*

Last came, and last did go,
The pilot of the Galilean lake;
Two massy keys he bore of metals twain
(The golden opes, the iron shuts amain[1]).
He shook his mitered locks, and stern bespake:—
"How well could I have spared for thee, young swain,
Enow of such as for their bellies' sake
Creep and intrude and climb into the fold!
Of other care they little reck'ning make
Than how to scramble at the shearers' feast
And shove away the worthy bidden guest.
Blind mouths! that scarce themselves know how to hold
A sheep-hook, or have learned aught else the least
That to the faithful herdsman's art belongs!

What recks it them? What need they? they are sped,[2]
And, when they list,[3] their lean and flashy songs
Grate on their scrannel piles of wretched straw;
The hungry sheep look up, and are not fed,
But, swoll'n with wind and the rank mist they draw,
Rot inwardly, and foul contagion spread;
Besides what the grim wolf with privy paw
Daily devours apace, and nothing said;
But that two-handed engine at the door
Stands ready to smite once, and smite no more."

John Milton
Lycidas: 'the ruin of our corrupted clergy'

1. *amain:* with force. 2. *sped:* prosperous. 3. *list:* so incline.

HOLY WILLIE'S PRAYER*

And send the godly in a pet to pray. —POPE

O Thou, that in the heavens does dwell,
Wha, as it pleases best Thysel',
Sends ane to heaven an' ten to hell,
        A' for thy glory,
And no for onie guid or ill
        They've done afore Thee!

I bless and praise Thy matchless might,
When thousands Thou hast left in night
That I am here afore Thy sight,
        For gifts an' grace
A burning and a shining light
        To a' this place.

What was I, or my generation,
That I should get sic exaltation,
I wha deserved most just damnation
   For broken laws,
Sax thousand years ere my creation,
   Thro' Adam's cause.

When from my mither's womb I fell,
Thou might hae plung'd me deep in hell,
To gnash my gooms, and weep and wail,
   In burnin lakes,
Where damnèd devils roar and yell,
   Chained to their stakes.

Yet I am here a chosen sample,
To show thy grace is great and ample;
I'm here a pillar o' Thy temple,
   Strong as a rock,
A guide, a buckler, and example,
   To a' Thy flock.

O Lord, Thou kens what zeal I bear,
When drinkers drink, an' swearers swear,
An' singing here, an' dancin' there,
   Wi' great and sma';
For I am keepit by Thy fear
   Free frae them a'.

But yet, O Lord! confess I must,
At times I'm fashed wi' fleshly lust:
An' sometimes, too, in warldly trust,
   Vile self gets in;
But Thou remembers we are dust,
   Defiled wi' sin.

O Lord! yestreen, Thou kens, wi' Meg—
Thy pardon I sincerely beg;
O! may't ne'er be a livin plague
      To my dishonour,
An' I'll ne'er lift a lawless leg
      Again upon her.

Besides, I farther maun allow,
Wi' Leezie's lass, three times I trow—
But Lord, that Friday I was fou,
      When I cam near her;
Or else, Thou kens, Thy servant true
      Wad never steer her.

Maybe Thou lets this fleshly thorn
Buffet Thy servant e'en and morn,
Lest he owre proud and high should turn,
      That he's sae gifted:
If sae, Thy han' maun e'en be borne,
      Until Thou lift it.

Lord, bless Thy chosen in this place,
For here Thou has a chosen race:
But God confound their stubborn face,
      An' blast their name,
Wha bring Thy elders to disgrace
      An' public shame.

Lord, mind Gaw'n Hamilton's deserts;
He drinks, an' swears, an' plays at cartes,
Yet has sae mony takin arts,
      Wi' great and sma',
Frae God's ain priest the people's hearts
      He steals awa.

An' when we chastened him therefor,
Thou kens how he bred sic a splore,[1]
An' set the warld in a roar
    O' laughing at us;—
Curse Thou his basket and his store,
    Kale an' potatoes.

Lord, hear my earnest cry and pray'r,
Against that Presbyt'ry o' Ayr;
Thy strong right hand, Lord, make it bare
    Upo' their heads;
Lord, visit them, an' dinna spare,
    For their misdeeds.

O Lord, my God! that glib-tongued Aiken,
My vera heart and flesh are quakin,
To think how we stood sweatin, shakin,
    An' pissed wi' dread,
While he, wi' hingin lip an' snakin,
    Held up his head.

Lord, in Thy day o' vengeance try him,
Lord, visit them wha did employ him,
And pass not in Thy mercy by them,
    Nor hear their pray'r,
But for thy people's sake destroy them,
    An' dinna spare.

But, Lord, remember me an' mine
Wi' mercies temporal and divine,
That I for grace an' gear may shine,
    Excelled by nane,
And a' the glory shall be thine,
    Amen, Amen!

Robert Burns

1. *splore:* prank, frolic.

ON THE SITE OF A MULBERRY-TREE PLANTED BY WILLIAM SHAKESPEARE, FELLED BY THE REV. F. GASTRELL

This tree, here fall'n, no common birth or death
Shared with its kind. The world's enfranchised son,
Who found the trees of Life and Knowledge one,
Here set it, frailer than his laurel-wreath.
Shall not the wretch whose hand it fell beneath
Rank also singly—the supreme unhung?
Lo! Sheppard, Turpin, pleading with black tongue
This viler thief's unsuffocated breath!
We'll search thy glossary, Shakespeare! whence almost,
And whence alone, some name shall be reveal'd
For this deaf drudge, to whom no length of ears
Sufficed to catch the music of the spheres;
Whose soul is carrion now,—too mean to yield
Some starveling's ninth allotment of a ghost.

Dante Gabriel Rossetti

BAGMAN O'REILLY'S CURSE*

I daresay that's the custom in your church:
You, seated, preached while I, the sinner, stood.
I thank you for this knowledge, Reverend Sir,
And for the lingering scent of your rich food.

Your charity of wind left me replete
With all the blessings I am notching here
Upon this stick with my small pocket knife
Beneath the moon, the mistress of the year.

I wish you coughing cows and withered corn,
Blood in your milk and scabies in your blood.
I wish you ten years' drought, and, when it rains,
A cold, persistent leak upon your bed.

May all your meals be burned, or underdone,
Your bacon taste of mildew, rats and smoke.
May your worst neighbours steal your finest bull,
Exhaust him, then castrate him for a joke.

May all the handles break off all your tools,
Or split and leave cruel splinters in your hand.
May every gun you buy kick like a horse
Yet never harm the birds that strip your land.

May both your daughters grow to look like you
And bear a crop of bastards by your son,
And may your wife grow teeth where never teeth
Grew in a woman since the world began,

Or rather, since the former would be no
More than is normal in your noble line,
And the latter, God forgive me, no great loss,
For you own cows and nany goats and swine,

This final wish I make, this final notch
(At every cut, the virgin sapwood bleeds)
When at last, well watered with your tears,
Milady's garden sprouts black widow's weeds

May I be seated where I can see down
Far down to where, chained in sow's muck, you lie
Attended by cold worms and hedgerow priests
More hungry and less merciful than I.

Les A. Murray

TO PIUS IX*

The cannon's brazen lips are cold;
  No red shell blazes down the air;
And street and tower, and temple old,
  Are silent as despair.

The Lombard stands no more at bay,
  Rome's fresh young life has bled in vain;
The ravens scattered by the day
  Come back with night again.

Now, while the fratricides of France
  Are treading on the neck of Rome,
Hider at Gaeta, seize thy chance!
  Coward and cruel, come!

Creep now from Naples' bloody skirt;
  Thy mummer's part was acted well,
While Rome, with steel and fire begirt,
  Before thy crusade fell!

Her death-groans answered to thy prayer
  Thy chant, the drum and bugle-call;
Thy lights, the burning villa's glare;
  Thy beads, the shell and ball!

Let Austria clear thy way, with hands
  Foul from Ancona's cruel sack,
And Naples, with his dastard bands
  Of murderers, lead thee back!

Rome's lips are dumb; the orphan's wail,
  The mother's shriek, thou mayst not hear

Above the faithless Frenchman's hail,
  The unsexed shaveling's cheer!

Go, bind on Rome her cast-off weight,
  The double curse of crook and crown,
Though woman's scorn and manhood's hate
  From wall and roof flash down!

Nor heed those blood-stains on the wall,
  Not Tiber's flood can wash away,
Where, in thy stately Quirinal,[1]
  Thy mangled victims lay!

Let the world murmur; let its cry
  Of horror and disgust be heard;
Truth stands alone; thy coward lie
  Is backed by lance and sword!

The cannon of St. Angelo,
  And chanting priest and clanging bell,
And beat of drum and bugle blow,
  Shall greet thy coming well!

Let lips of iron and tongues of slaves
  Fit welcome give thee; for her part,
Rome, frowning o'er her new-made graves,
  Shall curse thee from her heart!

No wreaths of sad Campagna's flowers
  Shall childhood in thy pathway fling;
No garlands from their ravaged bowers
  Shall Terni's maidens bring;

But, hateful as that tyrant old,
   The mocking witness of his crime,
In thee shall loathing eyes behold
   The Nero of our time!

Stand where Rome's blood was freest shed,
   Mock Heaven with impious thanks and call
Its curses on the patriot dead,
   Its blessings on the Gaul!

Or sit upon thy throne of lies,
   A poor, mean idol, blood-besmeared,
Whom even its worshippers despise,
   Unhonored, unrevered!

Yet, Scandal of the World! from thee
   One needful truth mankind shall learn:
That kings and priests to Liberty
   And God are false in turn.

Earth wearies of them; and the long
   Meek sufferance of the Heavens doth fail:
Woe for weak tyrants, when the strong
   Wake, struggle, and prevail!

Not vainly Roman hearts have bled
   To feed the Crosier and the Crown,
If, roused thereby, the world shall tread
   The twin-born vampires down!

John Greenleaf Whittier

1. *Quirinal:* Roman hill, site of a papal palace.

THE PILL

Must delicate women die in vain
While age confabulates? Not long
Ago, I knew and wept such wrong.
My favourite cousin, Ethelind,
Bewildered, shaking a head of curls,
Was gone at twenty-two, her babe
Unmothered—she had so little breath.
Now prelates in the Vatican
Are whispering from pillar to pillar
Examining in Latin the Pill,
Pessary, letter, cap. What can
We do until they have decreed
Their will, changing the ancient creed,
But lie awake on a separate pillow?
Now in a sky-tormented world,
These nightly watchers of the womb,
May bind archangels by the pinion,
As though they had dragged them down to marble
And bronze, dire figures of the past
That veil a young girl in her tomb.

Austin Clarke

EPITAPH

Posterity will ne'er survey
    A nobler grave than this:
Here lie the bones of Castlereagh:
    Stop, traveller, and piss.

George Gordon, Lord Byron

THE GENERAL

"Good morning; good morning!" the General said
When we met him last week on our way to the line.
Now the soldiers he smiled at are most of 'em dead,
And we're cursing his staff for incompetent swine.
"He's a cheery old card," grunted Harry to Jack
As they slogged up to Arras with rifle and pack.

*   *   *   *

But he did for them both with his plan of attack.

Siegfried Sassoon

VII.

POETS, CRITICS
& SCHOLARS

Who killed John Keats?
  "I," says the *Quarterly*,
So savage and Tartarly,
  "'Twas one of my feats."
                    GEORGE GORDON, Lord Byron

Get you to the hell you got your lame lines from,
Bad poets, clutterers of your age!
                    CATULLUS, XIV

SKELTON LAUREATE, DEFENDER, AGAINST LUSTY GARNESCHE, WELL-BESEEN[1] CHRISTOPHER, CHALLENGER

I have your lewd letter receivèd,
And well I have it perceivèd,
And your skrike[2] I have espièd,
That your mad mind contrivèd.
Saving your usher's rod,[3]
I cast me not to be odd
With neither of you twain:
Wherefore I write again
How the favour of your face
Is void of all good grace;
For all your carpet cushions,
Ye have knavish conditions.
Gup, marmoset, jast ye, morell![4]
I am laureate, I am no lorel.[5]
Lewdly your time ye spend
My living to reprehend;
And will never intend
Your own lewdness to amend:
Your English lewdly ye sort,
And falsely ye me report.
Garnesche, ye gape too wide:
Your knavery I will not hide,
For to assuage your pride.

When ye were younger of age
Ye were a kitchen-page,
A dish-washer, a drivel,
In the pot your nose did snivel;
Ye frièd and ye broilèd,
Ye roasted and ye boilèd,

Ye roasted, like a fon,[6]
A goose with the feet upon;
Ye sluffered up[7] souce
In my Lady Bruce's house.
Whereto should I write
Of such a greasy knight?
A bawdy dish-clout
That bringeth the world about
With hafting and with polling,[8]
With lying and controlling.

At Guines when ye were
But a slender spere,[9]
Deckèd lewdly in your gear;
For when ye dwelt there
Ye had a knavish coat
Was scantly worth a groat;
In dud frieze[10] ye were shrinèd
With better frieze linèd;
The outside every day,
Ye might no better a way;
The inside ye did call
Your best gown festivall.
Your drapery ye did want,
The ward with you was scant.
When ye cast a sheepës eye,
. . . .[11]Mistress Andelby,
. . . . Guines upon a gong,[12]
. . . . sat somewhat too long;
. . . . her husband's head
. . . . mall of lead,
. . . . that ye there preachèd,
To her love ye not reachèd:
Ye would have bussed her bum

So that she would have come
Unto your lousy den.
But she of all men
Had you most in despite,
Ye lost her favour quite;
Your pillèd-garlick head[13]
Could occupy there no stead;
She callèd you Sir Guy of Gaunt,
Nosèd like an elephaunt,
A pickaxe or a twible;[14]
She said how ye did bridle,
Much like a dromedary;
Thus with you she did wary,
With much matter more
That I keep in store.

Your breath is strong and quick;
Ye are an elder-stick;
Ye wot what I think—
At both ends ye stink.
Great danger for the king,
When his Grace is fastíng,
His presence to approach:
It is to your reproach.
It falleth for no swine,
Nor sowters,[15] to drink wine,
Nor such a noddipol[16]
A priest for to control.

Little wit in your scribës noll,[17]
That scribblèd your fond scroll,
Upon him for to take
Against me for to make,
Like a doctor dawpate,[18]

A laureate poet for to rate.
Your termes are too gross,
Too far from the purpose,
To contaminate
And to violate
The dignity laureate.

Bold bayard,[19] ye are too blind,
And grow all out of kind,
To occupy so your mind;
For reason can I none find
Nor good rhyme in your matter:
I wonder that ye smatter,
So for a knave to clatter!
Ye would be callèd a maker
And make much like Jake Raker;
Ye are a comely craker,[20]
Ye learnèd of some pie-baker!
Cast up your curious writing,
And your dirty inditing,
And your spiteful despiting,
For all is not worth a miting,[21]
A mackerel nor a whiting:
Had ye gone with me to school
And occupied no better your tool,
Ye should have kowthèd[22] me a fool.

But now, gawdy, greasy Garnesche,
Your face I wis to varnish
So surely it shall not tarnish.
Though a Saracen's head ye bear,
Rough and full of lousy hair,
As every man well seeth,
Full of great knavish teeth,

In a field of green peason,[23]
Is rhyme yet out of reason;
Your wit is so geson[24]
Ye rail all out of season.

    Your skin scabbèd and scurvy,
Tawny, tannèd, and shurvy;[25]
Now upon this heat
Rankly when ye sweat,
Men say ye will wax lousy,
Drunken, droopy, drowsy!
Your sword ye swear, I ween,
So trenchant and so keen,
Shall cut both white and green:[26]
Your folly is too great
The king's colours to threat.
Your breath it is so fell
And so puauntly[27] doth smell,
And so heinously doth stink,
That neither pump nor sink
Doth savour half so sour
Against a stormy shower.
O ladies of bright colóur,
Of beauty that beareth the floure,
When Garnesche cometh you among
With his breath so strong,
Without ye have a confectíon
Against his poisoned infectíon,
Else with his stinking jaws
He will cause you cast your craws,
And make your stomach seek
Over the perch to preke.[28]

    Now, Garnesche, guard thy gums,

My serpentines and my guns
Against ye now I bend;
Thyself therefore defend.
Thou toad, thou scorpion,
Thou bawdy babion,[29]
Thou bear, thou bristlèd boar,
Thou Moorish manticore,
Thou rammish stinking goat,
Thou foul churlish parrót,
Thou grisly Gorgon glaimy,[30]
Thou sweaty sloven seimy,
Thou murrion, thou mawment,[31]
Thou false stinking serpent,
Thou mockish marmoset,
I will not die in thy debt!
Tyburn[32] thou me assignèd,
Where *thou* shouldst have been shrinèd;
The next halter there shall be
I bequeath it whole to thee!
Such pilfery thou hast packèd,
And so thyself o'er-watchèd
That there thou shouldst be rackèd,
If thou were meetly matchèd.

Ye may well be bedawèd,
Ye are a fool outlawèd;
And for to tell the ground,
Pay Stokes his five pound.
I say, Sir Dalyrag,[33]
Ye bear you bold and brag
With other mennës charge:
Ye cut your cloth too large:
Such polling pageants ye play,
To point you fresh and gay.

And he that scribblèd your scrollës,
I reckon you in my rollës
For two drunken soulës.
Read and learn ye may
How old proverbës say,
That bird is not honést
That 'fileth his own nest.
If he wist what some wot,
The flesh basting of his coat
Was sowèd with slender threde.
God send you well good speed,
With *Dominus vobiscum!*
Good Latin for Jack-a-Thrum,[34]
Till more matter may come.
        By the King's most noble commandment.

                    John Skelton

1. *Well-beseen:* well-dressed, handsome. 2. *skrike:* screech or shriek? 3. *usher's rod:* Garnesche was gentleman-usher to Henry VIII. 4. *Gup, marmoset, jast ye, morell!* Giddyap, monkey, make haste, horse! 5. *lorel:* knave. 6. *fon:* fool. 7. *sluffered up:* gobbled noisily. 8. *hafting . . . polling:* swindling and plundering. 9. *spere:* stripling. 10. *dud frieze:* cloak of coarse woolen cloth. 11. The manuscript is torn here. 12. *gong:* privy. 13. *pillèd-garlick head:* bald head like peeled garlic. 14. *twible:* double-headed ax. 15. *sowters:* cobblers. 16. *noddipol:* blockhead, noodle. 17. *noll:* head. 18. *daw-pate:* simpleton. 19. *bayard:* bay horse. 20. *craker:* braggart. 21. *miting:* little creature. 22. *kowthèd:* known. 23. *peason:* peas. 24. *geson:* scanty. 25. *shurvy:* scurfy, scrofulous. 26. *white and green:* colors Skelton wore as laureate. 27. *puauntly:* stinkingly. 28. *Over the perch to preke:* hawking term: to preke off the perch means to topple off it; hence, in the case of Garnesche's stomach, to vomit. 29. *babion:* baboon. 30. *glaimy:* viscid or slimy. 31. *Thou murrion, thou mawment:* thou Moor, thou Mahomet (false prophet). 32. *Tyburn:* site of public executions. 33. *Sir Dalyrag:* the name suggests dalliance. 34. *Jack-a-Thrum:* probably, a trifling string-plucker.

UPON THE AUTHOR OF A PLAY CALLED SODOM*

Tell me, abandoned miscreant, prithee tell,
What damnèd pow'r, invoked and sent from Hell,
(If Hell were bad enough) did thee inspire
To write what fiends ashamed would blushing hear?
Hast thou of late embraced some succubus
And used the lewd familiar for a Muse,
Or didst thy soul by inch o' the candle sell
To gain the glorious name of pimp to Hell?
If so, go, and its vowed allegiance swear,
Without press-money be its volunteer:[1]
May he who envies thee deserve thy fate,
Deserve both Heav'n's and mankind's scorn and hate.
Disgrace to libels! Foil to very shame,
Whom 'tis a scandal to vouchsafe to damn!
What foul description's foul enough for thee,
Sunk quite below the reach of infamy?
Thou covet'st to be lewd, but want'st the might,
And art all-over devil but in wit.
Weak feeble strainer at mere ribaldry,
Whose Muse is impotent to that degree,
'T had need, like Age, be whipped to lechery.
Vile sot! who, clapped with poetry, art sick
And void'st corruption like a shankered prick.
Like ulcers, thy impostumed addle-brains
Drop out in matter which thy paper stains:
Whence nauseous rhymes by filthy births proceed,
As maggots, in some turd engend'ring, breed.
Thy Muse has got the flowers,[2] and they ascend
As in some green-sick girl, at upper end.
Sure Nature made—or meant at least t'have done 't—
Thy tongue a clitoris, thy mouth a cunt:
How well a dildo would that place become,
To gag it up, and make't forever dumb!

At least it should be syringed [or be seared,][3]
Or wear some stinking merkin[4] for a beard,
That all from its base converse might be scared,
As they a door shut up and marked *Beware*
That tells infection and the plague is there.
Thou Moorfields author, fit for bawds to quote
(If bawds themselves with honour safe may do 't)
When suburb 'prentice comes to hire delight
And wants incentives to dull appetite;
There punk,[5] perhaps, may thy brave works rehearse,
Frigging the senseless thing with hand and verse,
Which after shall (preferred to dressing-box)
Hold turpentine and medicines for the pox;
Or (if I may ordain a fate more fit)
For such foul, nasty excrements of wit,
May they condemned to the public jakes be lent,
(For me, I'd fear the piles in vengeance sent
Should I with them profane my fundament)
There bugger wiping porters when they shite,
And so thy book itself turn Sodomite.

John Oldham

1. *Without press-money be its volunteer:* join the army even without an enlistment bonus. 2. *flowers:* menstrual flow. 3. [*or be seared*]: the editor's guess. Three syllables are missing, perhaps dropped by Oldham's printer. 4. *merkin:* a pubic wig. 5. *punk:* harlot.

[OG]

Now stop your noses, Readers, all and some,
For here's a tun of midnight work to come,
Og[1] from a treason tavern rowling home.
Round as a globe, and liquored ev'ry chink,
Goodly and great, he sails behind his link;[2]

With all this bulk there's nothing lost in Og,
For ev'ry inch that is not fool is rogue:
A monstrous mass of foul corrupted matter,
As all the devils had spewed to make the batter.
When wine had given him courage to blaspheme,
He curses God, but God before cursed him;
And if man could have reason, none has more,
That made his paunch so rich and him so poor.
With wealth he was not trusted, for Heav'n knew
What 'twas of old to pamper up a Jew;
To what would he on quail and pheasant swell
That ev'n on tripe and carrion could rebel?
But though Heav'n made him poor (with rev'rence
    speaking),
He never was a poet of God's making;
The midwife laid her hand on his thick skull
With this prophetic blessing—"Be thou dull;
Drink, swear, and roar, forbear no lewd delight
Fit for thy bulk, do anything but write.
Thou art of lasting make, like thoughtless men,
A strong nativity—but for the pen;
Eat opium, mingle arsenic in thy drink,
Still thou mayst live, avoiding pen and ink."
I see, I see, 'tis counsel given in vain,
For treason botched in rhyme will be thy bane;
Rhyme is the rock on which thou art to wreck,
'Tis fatal to thy fame and to thy neck.
Why should thy metre good King David blast?
A psalm of his will surely be thy last.
Dar'st thou presume in verse to meet thy foes,
Thou whom the penny pamphlet foiled in prose?
Doeg,³ whom God for mankind's mirth has made,
O'er-tops thy talent in thy very trade;
Doeg to thee (thy paintings are so coarse)

A poet is, though he's the poet's horse.
A double noose thou on thy neck dost pull
For writing treason and for writing dull;
To die for faction is a common evil,
But to be hanged for nonsense is the devil.
Hadst thou the glories of thy King expressed,
Thy praises had been satire at the best;
But thou in clumsy verse, unlicked, unpointed,
Hast shamefully defied the Lord's anointed.
I will not rake the dunghill of thy crimes,
For who would read thy life that reads thy rhymes?
But of King David's foes be this the doom:
May all be like the young man Absalom;
And for my foes may this their blessing be:
To talk like Doeg and to write like thee.

John Dryden
Absalom and Achitophel

1. *Og:* Thomas Shadwell. 2. *link:* torch. 3. *Doeg:* Elkanah Settle.

ON BURNING A DULL POEM

Written in the year 1729

An ass's hoof alone can hold
That pois'nous juice which kills by cold.
Methought when I this poem read
No vessel but an ass's head
Such frigid fustian could contain;
I mean the head without the brain.
The cold conceits, the chilling thoughts,

Went down like stupefying draughts:
I found my head began to swim,
A numbness crept through ev'ry limb.
In haste, with imprecations dire,
I threw the volume in the fire,
When—who could think—though cold as ice,
It burnt to ashes in a trice.

How could I more enhaunce its fame?
Though born in snow, it died in flame.

Jonathan Swift

[ATTICUS]

How did they[1] fume, and stamp, and roar, and chafe!
And swear, not Addison himself was safe.
   Peace to all such! but were there one whose fires
True genius kindles, and fair fame inspires;
Blest with each talent, and each art to please,
And born to write, converse, and live with ease,
Should such a man, too fond to rule alone,
Bear, like the Turk, no brother near the throne,
View him with scornful, yet with jealous eyes,
And hate for arts that caused himself to rise;
Damn with faint praise, assent with civil leer,
And, without sneering, teach the rest to sneer;
Willing to wound, and yet afraid to strike,
Just hint a fault, and hesitate dislike;
Alike reserved to blame, or to commend,
A timorous foe, and a suspicious friend;
Dreading e'en fools, by flatterers besieged,

And so obliging, that he ne'er obliged;
Like Cato, give his little Senate laws,
And sit attentive to his own applause:
While wits and Templars every sentence raise,
And wonder with a foolish face of praise—
Who but must laugh, if such a man there be?
Who would not weep, if Atticus[2] were he?

Alexander Pope
An Epistle from Mr. Pope to Dr. Arbuthnot

1. *they:* dull versifiers. 2. *Atticus:* Joseph Addison.

ON THE EDITION OF MR. POPE'S WORKS
WITH A COMMENTARY AND NOTES

In evil hour did Pope's declining age,
Deceived and dazzled by the tinsel show
Of wordy science and the nauseous flow
Of mean officious flatteries, engage
Thy venal quill to deck his laboured page
With ribald nonsense, and permit to strew,
Amidst his flowers, the baleful weeds, that grow
In the unblessed soil of rude and rancorous rage.
Yet this the avenging Muse ordained so,
When, by his counsel or weak sufferance,
To thee were trusted Shakespeare's fame and fate:
She doomed him down the stream of time to tow
Thy foul, dirt-loaded hulk, or sink perchance,
Dragged to oblivion by the foundering weight.

Thomas Edwards

EPIGRAM ON ELPHINSTONE'S TRANSLATION
OF MARTIAL'S EPIGRAMS

O thou whom Poetry abhors,
Whom Prose has turnèd out of doors,
Heard'st thou yon groan?—proceed no further,
'Twas laurel'd Martial calling murther.

Robert Burns

ALAS! 'TIS VERY SAD TO HEAR

Alas! 'tis very sad to hear,
You and your Muse's end draws near:
I only wish, if this be true,
To lie a little way from you.
The grave is cold enough for me
Without you and your poetry.

Walter Savage Landor

TO EDWARD FITZGERALD*

I chanced upon a new book yesterday:
I opened it, and, where my finger lay
    'Twixt page and uncut page, these words I read
—Some six or seven at most—and learned thereby
That you, FitzGerald, whom by ear and eye
    She never knew, "thanked Gòd my wife was dead."

Ay dead! and were yourself alive, good Fitz,
How to return your thanks would task my wits:
Kicking you seems the common lot of curs—
While more appropriate greeting lends you grace:
Surely to spit there glorifies your face—
Spitting—from lips once sanctified by Hers.

Robert Browning

THE HEART OF THOMAS HARDY

The heart of Thomas Hardy flew out of Stinsford churchyard.
A little thumping fig, it rocketed over the elm trees.
Lighter than air it flew straight to where its Creator
Waited in golden nimbus, just as in eighteen sixty,
Hardman and son of Brum had depicted Him in the chancel.
Slowly out of the grass, slitting the mounds in the centre,
Riving apart the roots, rose the new covered corpses
Tess and Jude and His Worship, various unmarried mothers,
Woodmen, cutters of turf, adulterers, church restorers,
Turning aside the stones thump on the upturned churchyard.
Soaring over the elm trees slower than Thomas Hardy,
Weighted down with a Conscience, now for the first time fleshly,
Taking form as a growth hung from the feet like a sponge-bag.
There, in the heart of the nimbus, twittered the heart of Hardy.
There, on the edge of the nimbus, slowly revolved the corpses
Radiating around the twittering heart of Hardy,
Slowly started to turn in the light of their own Creator,
Died away in the night as frost will blacken a dahlia.

John Betjeman

ONE POET VISITS ANOTHER

His car was worth a thousand pounds and more,
A tall and glossy black silk hat he wore;
His clothes were pressed, like pretty leaves, when they
Are found in Bibles closed for many a day;
Until the birds I loved dropped something that—
    As white as milk, but thick as any cream—
Went pit, pit, pat! Right on his lovely hat!

*   *   *

Lead this unhappy poet to his car—
    Where is his longing now, where his desire?
When left alone, I'll ride him to his grave,
    On my own little horse of wind and fire.

                                        W. H. Davies

DULCE ET DECORUM EST*

Bent double, like old beggars under sacks,
Knock-kneed, coughing like hags, we cursed through sludge,
Till on the haunting flares we turned our backs
And towards our distant rest began to trudge.
Men marched asleep. Many had lost their boots
But limped on, blood-shod. All went lame; all blind;
Drunk with fatigue; deaf even to the hoots
Of tired, outstripped Five-Nines[1] that dropped behind.

Gas! Gas! Quick, boys!—An ecstasy of fumbling,
Fitting the clumsy helmets just in time;
But someone still was yelling out and stumbling
And flound'ring like a man in fire or lime . . .

Dim, through the misty panes and thick green light,
As under a green sea, I saw him drowning.

In all my dreams, before my helpless sight,
He plunges at me, guttering, choking, drowning.

If in some smothering dreams you too could pace
Behind the wagon that we flung him in,
And watch the white eyes writhing in his face,
His hanging face, like a devil's sick of sin;
If you could hear, at every jolt, the blood
Come gargling from the froth-corrupted lungs,
Obscene as cancer, bitter as the cud
Of vile, incurable sores on innocent tongues,—
My friend, you would not tell with such high zest
To children ardent for some desperate glory,
The old Lie: Dulce et decorum est
Pro patria mori.

Wilfred Owen

1. *Five-Nines:* gas shells.

'BUSBY, WHOSE VERSE NO PIERCING BEAMS, NO RAYS'

Busby, whose verse no piercing beams, no rays
can penetrate, whom dark dogmas enchant
to speak in tongues, all telling us you can't
live without Christ and critical essays—
come, pour the whiskey, swell your tongue and glaze
your eye with eloquence, until I grant
your greatness, who so gorgeously can rant
at the sick world, which will not pay, nor praise.

Is there no place, then, where the sacred tongue
can buzz in magazines—flies on the dung
which spreads to fertilize the fallow masses?
Then try the quarterlies: moving among
the select few, still willing to be stung,
they trot the field, lofty as horses' asses.

Richard Moore

TO THE REVIEWERS

What is a modern Poet's fate?
To write his thoughts upon a slate:—
The Critic spits on what is done,—
Gives it a wipe,—and all is gone.

Thomas Hood

THE CURSE

To a sister of an enemy of the author's who disapproved of "The Playboy"

Lord, confound this surly sister,
Blight her brow with blotch and blister,
Cramp her larynx, lung, and liver,
In her guts a galling give her.

Let her live to earn her dinners
In Mountjoy[1] with seedy sinners:
Lord, this judgment quickly bring.
And I'm Your servant, J. M. Synge.

John Millington Synge

1. *Mountjoy:* prison in Dublin.

VALENTINE*

For a Mr. Lee Wilson Dodd and Any of His Friends Who Want It.

Sing a song of critics
pockets full of lye
four and twenty critics
hope that you will die
hope that you will peter out
hope that you will fail
so they can be the first one
be the first to hail
any happy weakening or sign of quick decay.
(All are very much alike, weariness too great,
sordid small catastrophes, stack the cards on fate,
very vulgar people, annals of the callous,
dope fiends, soldiers, prostitutes,
men without a gallus*)
If you do not like them lads
one thing you can do
stick them up your asses lads
My Valentine to you.
* . . . .

Ernest Hemingway

PIPLING

Behold the critic, pitched like the *castrati*,
Imperious youngling, though approaching forty;
He heaps few honors on a living head;
He loves himself, and the illustrious dead;
He pipes, he squeaks, he quivers through his nose,—
Some cannot praise him: *I* am one of those.

Theodore Roethke

THE CRITIC ON THE HEARTH

When Wallaby would come to call on me,
He'd cock his little paws into a prance
Arrested in thin air, and take a stance
(Not easy, when in session by my hob
And rapt in the ignition of his cob)
As one who waters the green seedling young
With wisdom's outfall, the thick ramping sum
Of many tributary years, now come
To a grey head and splurged to purchase new
Shoots, blooms, shucks, fruit, and finally seeds, too.
But when his voice came out of leonine
Dewlaps, it was a fluted, epicene
Column of footnotes, all italicized,
That rose and rose until capitalized
By an ornate Corinthian device
Framed in the hypersonic tones of mice.
Well, that was Conrad Wallaby, the great
Tweed-bearing critic, piped and ungulate
In Pannish season, otherwise well shod
In the high-button shoes of the hard god
Of our feared fathers, ordinately fond
Of donnish wit deliberately donned,
Of shag and tepid tankards of brown ale,
Of company preponderantly male,
Of oolong tea, cress sandwiches, and pale
Dry sherry, port and nuts, dear Major Grey's,
Of good long reads in Doyle on rainy days,
Of a small income herited like genes,
Of living just beyond his patrons' means,
Of loving Art and Beauty and the stones
Of Venice and the venerated bones

Enclosèd here, of quips and cranks and wiles
Arch and archaic, nods and becks and smiles,
Of passion and expression sweetly linked.
Thank God the silly bastard is extinct.

L. E. Sissman

TO MY LEAST FAVORITE REVIEWER

When I was young, just starting at our game,
I ambitioned to be christlike, and forgive thee.
For a mortal Jew that proved too proud an aim;
Now it's my humbler hope just to outlive thee.

Howard Nemerov

ON PHILOSOPHERS*

Lofty-brow-flourishers,
   Nose-in-beard-wallowers,
Bag-and-beard-nourishers,
   Dish-and-all-swallowers,
Old-cloak-investitors,
   Barefoot-look-fashioners,
Night-private-feast-takers,
   Craft-lucubrationers,
Youth-cheaters, word-catchers, vain-glory-osophers,
Such are your seekers of virtue Philosophers.

Anonymous
English, ca. 1600

EPIGRAM ON THE REFUSAL OF THE UNIVERSITY OF OXFORD TO SUBSCRIBE TO HIS TRANSLATION OF HOMER

Could Homer come himself, distressed and poor,
And tune his harp at Rhedicina's door,
The rich old vixen would exclaim (I fear),
Begone! no tramper gets a farthing here.

William Cowper

LINES TO A DON

Remote and ineffectual Don
That dared attack my Chesterton,
With that poor weapon, half-impelled,
Unlearnt, unsteady, hardly held,
Unworthy for a tilt with men—
Your quavering and corroded pen;
Don poor at Bed and worse at Table,
Don pinched, Don starved, Don miserable;
Don stuttering, Don with roving eyes,
Don nervous, Don of crudities;
Don clerical, Don ordinary,
Don self-absorbed and solitary;
Don here-and-there, Don epileptic;
Don puffed and empty, Don dyspeptic;
Don middle-class, Don sycophantic,
Don dull, Don brutish, Don pedantic;
Don hypocritical, Don bad,
Don furtive, Don three-quarters mad;
Don (since a man must make an end),
Don that shall never be my friend.

Don different from those regal Dons!
With hearts of gold and lungs of bronze,
Who shout and bang and roar and bawl
The Absolute across the hall,
Or sail in amply bellowing gown
Enormous through the Sacred Town,
Bearing from College to their homes
Deep cargoes of gigantic tomes;
Dons admirable! Dons of Might!
Uprising on my inward sight
Compact of ancient tales, and port
And sleep—and learning of a sort.
Dons English, worthy of the land;
Dons rooted; Dons that understand.
Good Dons perpetual that remain
A landmark, walling in the plain—
The horizon of my memories—
Like large and comfortable trees.

Don very much apart from these,
Thou scapegoat Don, thou Don devoted,
Don to thine own damnation quoted,
Perplexed to find thy trivial name
Reared in my verse to lasting shame.
Don dreadful, rasping Don and wearing,
Repulsive Don—Don past all bearing,
Don of the cold and doubtful breath,
Don despicable, Don of death;
Don nasty, skimpy, silent, level;
Don evil; Don that serves the devil.
Don ugly—that makes fifty lines.
There is a Canon which confines
A Rhymed Octosyllabic Curse
If written in Iambic Verse

To fifty lines. I never cut;
I far prefer to end it—but
Believe me I shall soon return.
My fires are banked, but still they burn
To write some more about the Don
That dared attack my Chesterton.

Hilaire Belloc

ELEGY FOR A BAD POET,
TAKEN FROM US NOT LONG SINCE

"About the dead, no murmur of dispraise."
Who, me? I'm on my knees. Been there for days.
"Who, *you*?" To praise the Lord, His gracious ways.

John Frederick Nims

EMINENT CRITIC

"For each man kills the thing he loves"—it's true.
He, loving poetry, did what lovers do
To the fair body. I can't say he bettered it.
I only say he sure as hell four-lettered it.

John Frederick Nims

FOR AN EARLY RETIREMENT

Chinless and slouched, gray-faced, and slack of jaw,
Here plods depressed Professor Peckinpaugh,
Whose verse J. Donald Adams found "exciting."
This fitted him to teach Creative Writing.

Donald Hall

LINES ON BEING REFUSED A GUGGENHEIM FELLOWSHIP*

What curses should I choose?
What curses would a muse choose
If she had been, as I have been, refused,
Muse?
I need heroic tropes and sounding brass
To blast them that saw fit me not to pass.
And with the brass I need a sad bassoon
To play a soft, frail, melancholy tune;
For scorn and sorrow equally contend
In friendless me to be my only friend.
And I must, to be true to my debris,
Make of it both loss and victory.
Will you help me, will you from the Mount
Descend, and deign to take on my account?

Thank you.
Now my wing roots sprout again
Where Guggenheim and all his monied men
Unhinged me and me grounded with, they said,
Regret. Regret? Form letters no tears shed.
Nor was there any word from them of solace
As they their noes and noses turned in flawless
Admin-ese (the dialect
Of social workers, deans and savants wrecked),
Except that I was commonplace, since hordes
Went, by the same form letter, by the boards.
—Alas, that I filled out the application,
And waited six long months for my deflation.
Alas, that I told friends and blew my horn.
Alas, that I (or Guggenheim) was born.
Let me go to Lear's old blasted heath

And on the world's foundations whet my teeth.
And yet, by God, this last alas is wrong.

I come now to the part where Lycid's song
Changes, like a record, hot to sweet,
And all the lambs renew their beauteous bleat,
So that the hero, once deject, may twitch
His mantle, shove off and grow rich.
For why should I, free, white and thirty-eight,
Ask for help from some old passing plate?
Had I had the bad luck to be chosen,
These immortal lines would have been frozen
Into paragraphs of thanks as flat as those
Of sorrow which, as stated, me unchose.
And I'd have had my name among the scholars
Who study gews and gaws for Guggy's dollars
(Or Hank's or John's or Andy's, for that matter—
The cooking's not important; 'tis the batter).
And so I'll not regret my sour grapes,
Nor hold my peace, nor pull my gibes and japes,
Nor say alas that I can only rhyme on
Censures of, not praises of, Saint Simon.

Reed Whittemore

EPILOGUE

"Voici le temps des Assassins"—RIMBAUD

My bibliography has grown
   more slow
   than socialism in Ohio.
My teaching lacks the frigid gentility
   of the Harvard faery.

My syllabi lie
    upon my charity
    like grades
    upon a women's dormitory.
I have not walked in elevated clothes
    in Bascom's pews.
My shoes are dull;
    my tie askew.
My socks have holes
    unseen by soles.
Throughout the summer I stay pale.
I am not even "Yale."

But every year returns
    a moment for promotions,
    a time of defecations and defections,
    an hour of lopping and chopping.
They smile, drop the ax,
Let the scholars up or, mostly, out.
I smile, shake hands and pack.

Now is the month of June,
    the month of nature's clout.
Algae fills the pretty lakes.
Flies and beetles settle
    on the typewriter's rattle.
Heat descends.
Pay ends.
Ho hum.
Good-by,
    scum.

Dallas Wiebe

ACADEMIC CURSE: AN EPITAPH

Curse him who digs in yellow leaves
  To scrape my twisted tongue
Of twisted songs that once I sang
  Out of a twisted lung!

Rot take the worm that eats my dust.
  May his bowels wither!
I shall see him eat my words
  When he grovels hither.

Wesli Court

LETTER TO A LIBRARIAN

Mr. P.—I have heard it rumored
That you, humanist, librarian with a license,
In the shady privacy of your glassed room
Tore up my book of poems.

Sir, a word in your ear. Others
Have tried that game: burned Mann
And my immortal kinsman Heine.
Idiots! What act could be vainer?

For this act of yours, the ligatures
Pest-corroded, your eyes shall fall
From their sockets; drop on your lacquered desk
With the dull weight of pinballs.

And brighter than the sapless vine
Your hands shall flare;

To the murkiest kimbos of the library
Flashing my name like a neon sign.

And the candid great
Of whom not one was ever an Australian
Cry dustily from their shelves,
'Imposter! False custodian!'

Till a stunned derelict
You fall down blind, ear-beleaguered,
While Rabelais pipes you to a wished-for death
On a kazoo quaint and silvered.

Irving Layton

VIII.

OFFENDING RACE OF HUMANKIND

I am not in the least provoked at the sight of a lawyer, a pickpocket, a colonel, a fool, a lord, a gamester, a politician, a whoremonger, a physician, an evidence, a suborner, an attorney, a traitor, or the like: this is all according to the due course of things; but when I behold a lump of deformity and diseases both in body and mind, smitten with *pride*, it immediately breaks all the measures of my patience.

JONATHAN SWIFT, *Gulliver's Travels*

Were I (who to my cost already am
One of those strange, prodigious creatures, man)
A spirit free to choose, for my own share,
What case of flesh and blood I pleased to wear,
I'd be a dog, a monkey, or a bear,
Or anything but that vain animal
Who is so proud of being rational.

JOHN WILMOT, EARL OF ROCHESTER,
"A Satire against Reason and Mankind"

[TIMON CURSES ATHENS AND MANKIND]

Scene: Without the walls of Athens. Enter Timon.

Let me look back upon thee, O thou wall
That girdles in those wolves, dive in the earth
And fence not Athens! Matrons, turn incontinent!
Obedience fail in children! Slaves and fools,
Pluck the grave wrinkled Senate from the bench
And minister in their [steads]! To general filths
Convert o' th' instant green virginity!
Do't in your parents' eyes! Bankrupts, hold fast;
Rather than render back, out with your knives
And cut your trusters' throats! Bound servants,
    steal!
Large-handed robbers your grave masters are
And pill by law. Maid, to thy master's bed;
Thy mistress is o' th' brothel! Son of sixteen,
Pluck the lin'd crutch from thy old limping sire;
With it beat out his brains! Piety, and fear,
Religion to the gods, peace, justice, truth,
Domestic awe, night-rest, and neighbourhood,
Instruction, manners, mysteries, and trades,
Degrees, observances, customs, and laws,
Decline to your confounding contraries,
And [let] confusion live! Plagues incident to men,
Your potent and infectious fevers heap
On Athens, ripe for stroke! Thou cold sciatica,
Cripple our senators, that their limbs may halt
As lamely as their manners! Lust and liberty
Creep in the minds and marrows of our youth,
That 'gainst the stream of virtue they may strive,

And drown themselves in riot! Itches, blains,
Sow all th' Athenian bosoms; and their crop

Be general leprosy! Breath infect breath,
That their society, as their friendship, may
Be merely poison! Nothing I'll bear from thee
But nakedness, thou detestable town!
Take thou that too, with multiplying bans!
Timon will to the woods, where he shall find
Th' unkindest beast more kinder than mankind.
The gods confound—hear me, you good gods all,
Th' Athenians both within and out that wall!
And grant, as Timon grows, his hate may grow
To the whole race of mankind, high and low!
Amen.

William Shakespeare
Timon of Athens, IV, i

TIMON SPEAKS TO A DOG

Ah, dog. Here is my boot. Does it stink good?
For grub, no doubt, you'd say so. But I've none.
Grub elsewhere, dog. You've no time left for me.

Dogged sincerity maps out your face,
Tongue lolling out—you mean it, dog, you do!
Soft soggy eyes muddling up to mine—
Try probing higher than your belly's stint,
Dog, walk on two legs, upright, do.

Young business dog beneath a bowler hat
Pimpled and pink and swelling—dog the footsteps
Of some pin-striped dictator to your board

—They'll lodge you there, dog, crouch
   respectfully.
And don dog teach—teach what you've just been
   taught,
Regurgitate, then lick your vomit up,
Sit down, sit up, look bright, up dog and beg.
Hungry sheep look up? Hard lines on them.
Worry them, they'll never worry you.

God's your dog, young chaplain. You've a receipt
Worth ten. No cure of souls but fun and games.
Rescue dead sticks with gusto, master sees.
Sniff out holes Buber missed, master's there.
Bury your bone gods deep, don't dig it up.
Bear an illustrious mitre to your lord.
The good chap gets the stick, the bone goes free.
Try resurrection, bone. No good? Too bad.

Dogs don't lead, they follow. On a lead.
Are wolves around? Nice dog, you say to them.
Next best thing, say no wolves. Dogs believe
If men don't. And your congregants are dogs.
Dogs can be trained to love you. We love them—
That's why. Affection strongest when well bought.
Unswerving loyalty—get to the top
By doing what you're told. When at the top
What can you do but what dogs did before?
Where one shits all will shit. That pampered hound
Who licks your lily chops would, once you're down,
Bite the very tongue out of your head.
So much for man's best friend. Fawn as you will,
The muzzle hides the charge. Circle all night
The first bite wins the morning. Bye-bye dog.

I tuck my long-drawn tail into my coat
Trusting no dog sees. Pull my gloves
Over my blunted paws. My whiskers should
Hide my trusty button of a nose,
My peaked cap maudlin eyes, as back I go,
Dog, to my manger packed with doggish goods—
Tape recorders, books, enormous fires,
Plenty of food and drink, things in the post
Which, dog, make me feel good.

   Where is that bone?
I lost it long ago. It had no flesh,
No need, you'd say, for living. So it lived,
So grew, so spanned the sky, while I sniffed dung,
Following my doggy ends to doggy end.

Philip Hobsbaum

[SATAN BEHOLDS ADAM AND EVE IN EDEN]

O Hell! what do mine eyes with grief behold!
Into our room of bliss thus high advanced
Creatures of other mold, earth-born perhaps,
Not spirits, yet to heav'nly spirits bright
Little inferior; whom my thoughts pursue
With wonder, and could love, so lively shines
In them divine resemblance and such grace
The hand that formed them on their shape hath poured.
Ah gentle pair, ye little think how nigh
Your change approaches, when all these delights
Will vanish and deliver ye to woe,
More woe, the more your taste is now of joy;
Happy, but for so happy ill secured

Long to continue, and this high seat your Heav'n
Ill fenced for Heav'n to keep out such a foe
As now is entered; yet no purposed foe
To you whom I could pity thus forlorn,
Though I unpitied. League with you I seek
And mutual amity so strait, so close,
That I with you must dwell, or you with me
Henceforth; my dwelling haply may not please
Like this fair Paradise, your sense, yet such
Accept your Maker's work; he gave it me,
Which I as freely give; Hell shall unfold,
To entertain you two, her widest gates
And send forth all her kings; there will be room,
Not like these narrow limits, to receive
Your numerous offspring; if no better place,
Thank him who puts me loath to this revenge
On you who wrong me not, for him who wronged.
And should I at your harmless innocence
Melt, as I do, yet public reason just,
Honor and empire with revenge enlarged
By conquering this new world, compels me now
To do what else though damned I should abhor.

John Milton
Paradise Lost, IV

THE DAY OF JUDGMENT

Once, with a whirl of thought oppressed,
I sunk from reverie to rest.
An horrid vision seized my head,
I saw the graves give up their dead!
Jove, armed with terrors, burst the skies

And thunder roars, and lightning flies!
Confused, amazed, its fate unknown,
The world stands trembling at his throne!
While each pale sinner hangs his head,
Jove, nodding, shook the heavens, and said:
"Offending race of human kind,
By nature, custom, learning, blind;
You who, through frailty, slipped aside;
And you who never fell—through pride;
And you by differing churches shammed,
Who come to see each other damned
(So some folks told you, but they knew
No more of Jove's designs than you);
The world's mad business now is o'er,
And I resent these pranks no more.
I to such blockheads set my wit!
I damn such fools!—Go, go, you're *bit*."[1]

Jonathan Swift

1. *bit:* beaten, outwitted (slang).

SAM HALL*

Oh, my name it is Sam Hall, it is Sam Hall,
Yes, my name it is Sam Hall, it is Sam Hall;
Yes, my name it is Sam Hall, and I hate you one and all,
Yes, I hate you one and all, God damn your eyes.

Oh, I killed a man, they say, so they say;
Yes, I killed a man, they say, so they say;
I beat him on the head, and I left him there for dead,
Yes, I left him there for dead, God damn his eyes.

Oh, the parson he did come, he did come,
Yes, the parson he did come, he did come;
And he looked so bloody glum, as he talked of Kingdom Come—
He can kiss my ruddy bum, God damn his eyes.

And the sheriff he came too, he came too;
Yes, the sheriff he came too, he came too;
Yes, the sheriff he came too, with his men all dressed in blue—
Lord, they were a bloody crew, God damn their eyes.

Now up the rope I go, up I go;
Yes, up the rope I go, up I go;
And those bastards down below, they'll say, "Sam, we told you so,"
They'll say, "Sam, we told you so," God damn their eyes.

I saw my Nellie dressed in blue, dressed in blue;
I saw my Nellie in the crowd, all dressed in blue:
Says my Nellie, dressed in blue: "Your triflin' days are through—
Now I know that you'll be true, God damn your eyes."

And now in heaven I dwell, in heaven I dwell,
Yes, now in heaven I dwell, in heaven I dwell;
Yes, now in heaven I dwell—Holy Christ! It is a sell—
All the whores are down in hell, God damn their eyes.

Anonymous

British popular song, late eighteenth century; American version, 1930 or earlier

GOOD FRIDAY

You love us yet? Then really, what a One!
Now that the hustling, hooting, horror's done,
Popped in our pouch of spit, a hot-cross bun.

John Frederick Nims

'GOOD CREATURES, DO YOU LOVE YOUR LIVES'

Good creatures, do you love your lives
    And have you ears for sense?
Here is a knife like other knives,
    That cost me eighteen pence.

I need but stick it in my heart
    And down will come the sky,
And earth's foundations will depart
    And all you folk will die.

A. E. Housman

THE COMPLETE MISANTHROPIST

I love to think of things I hate
    In moments of mopishness;
I hate people who sit up straight,
And youths who smirk about their "date,"
    And the dates who smirk no less.

I hate children who clutch and whine,
    And the arrogant, virtuous poor;
And critical connoisseurs of wine,
And everything that is called a shrine,
    And Art and Literature.

I hate eggs and I hate the hen;
    I hate the rooster, too.
I hate people who wield the pen,
I hate women and I hate men;
    And what's more, I hate you.

Morris Bishop

THE HUSTLER*

The name of the game is beat the lame,
Take a woman and make her live in shame.

It makes no difference how much she scream or holler,
'Cause dope is my heaven and my God the
            almighty dollar.

I, the Hustler, swear by God
I would kill Pope Paul if pressed too hard,

I would squash out Bobby and do Jackie harm
And for one goddamn dollar would break her arm.

I, the Hustler, kick ass morning, noon, and night,
I would challenge Cassius and Liston to a fight.

I would climb in the ring with nothing but two P-.38's
And send either one that moved through the
            pearly gates.

I, the Hustler, can make Astaire dance and
            Sinatra croon,
And I would make the Supreme Court eat shit from
            a spoon.

Anonymous
Black American folk poem, ca. 1965

ANIMALS ARE PASSING FROM OUR LIVES

It's wonderful how I jog
on four honed-down ivory toes
my massive buttocks slipping
like oiled parts with each light step.

I'm to market. I can smell
the sour, grooved block, I can smell
the blade that opens the hole
and the pudgy white fingers

that shake out the intestines
like a hankie. In my dreams
the snouts drool on the marble,
suffering children, suffering flies,

suffering the consumers
who won't meet their steady eyes
for fear they could see. The boy
who drives me along believes

that any moment I'll fall
on my side and drum my toes
like a typewriter or squeal
and shit like a new housewife

discovering television,
or that I'll turn like a beast
cleverly to hook his teeth
with my teeth. No. Not this pig.

Philip Levine

SHITTY

Look thy last on all things shitty
   While thou'rt at it: soccer stars,
Soccer crowds, bedizened bushheads
   Jerking over their guitars,

German tourists, plastic roses,
   Face of Mao and face of Ché,
Women wearing curtains, blankets,
   Beckett at the I C A,

High-rise blocks and action paintings,
   Sculptures made from wire and lead:
Each of them a sight more lovely
   Than the screens around your bed.

Kingsley Amis

IX.

DAMNED
ABSTRACTIONS

Thanne come Slothe al bislabered with two slymy eiyen . . .
WILLIAM LANGLAND, *Piers Plowman*

Hatred of absolute rule, where will of one
Is law for all, and of that barren pride
In them who, by immunities unjust,
Between the sovereign and the people stand,
His helper and not theirs, laid stronger hold
Daily upon me . . .
WILLIAM WORDSWORTH, *The Prelude*

An intellectual hatred is the worst,
So let her think opinions are accursed.
WILLIAM BUTLER YEATS, "A Prayer for My Daughter"

To me, still, all abstractions smell . . .
DR. JOSEPH GOEBBELS in W. D. Snodgrass's
The Führer Bunker

CANTO XLV*

With usura hath no man a house of good stone
each block cut smooth and well fitting
that design might cover their face,
with usura
hath no man a painted paradise on his church wall
harpes et luthes
or where virgin receiveth message
and halo projects from incision,
with usura
seeth no man Gonzaga his heirs and his concubines
no picture is made to endure nor to live with
but it is made to sell and sell quickly
with usura, sin against nature,
is thy bread ever more of stale rags
is thy bread dry as paper,
with no mountain wheat, no strong flour
with usura the line grows thick
with usura is no clear demarcation
and no man can find site for his dwelling.
Stone cutter is kept from his stone
weaver is kept from his loom
WITH USURA
wool comes not to market
sheep bringeth no gain with usura
Usura is a murrain, usura
blunteth the needle in the maid's hand
and stoppeth the spinner's cunning. Pietro Lombardo
came not by usura
Duccio came not by usura
nor Pier della Francesca; Zuan Bellin' not by usura
nor was 'La Calunnia' painted.
Came not by usura Angelico; came not Ambrogio Praedis,

Came no church of cut stone signed: *Adamo me fecit.*
Not by usura St Trophime
Not by usura Saint Hilaire,
Usura rusteth the chisel
It rusteth the craft and the craftsman
It gnaweth the thread in the loom
None learneth to weave gold in her pattern;
Azure hath a canker by usura; cramoisi is unbroidered
Emerald findeth no Memling
Usura slayeth the child in the womb
It stayeth the young man's courting
It hath brought palsey to bed, lyeth
between the young bride and her bridegroom
      CONTRA NATURUM
They have brought whores for Eleusis
Corpses are set to banquet
at behest of usura.

Ezra Pound

[ENVY]*

Malicious Envy rode
Upon a ravenous wolf, and still did chaw
Between his cankered teeth a venemous toad,
That all the poison ran about his chaw;[1]
But inwardly he chawèd his own maw[2]
At neighbours' wealth, that made him ever sad;
For death it was, when any good he saw,
And wept, that cause of weeping none he had,
But when he heard of harm, he wexèd wondrous glad.

All in a kirtle of discoloured say[3]

He clothèd was, ypainted full of eyes;
And in his bosom secretly there lay
An hateful snake, the which his tail upties
In many folds, and mortal sting implies.
Still as he rode, he gnashed his teeth to see
Those heaps of gold with griple[4] covetise,
And grudgèd at the great felicity
Of proud Lucifera, and his own company.

He hated all good works and virtuous deeds,
And him no less, that any like did use,
And who with gracious bread the hungry feeds,
His alms for want of faith he doth accuse;
So every good to bad he doth abuse:
And eke[5] the verse of famous poets' wit
He does backbite, and spiteful poison spews
From leprous mouth on all that ever writ:
Such one vile Envy was, that fifte in row did sit.

Edmund Spenser
The Faerie Queene, I, iv

1. *chaw:* chops. 2. *maw:* guts. 3. *kirtle of discoloured say:* motley-colored woolen coat or tunic. 4. *griple:* greedy. 5. *eke:* also.

TO DETRACTION I PRESENT MY POESIE

Foul canker of fair virtuous action,
Vile blaster of the freshest blooms on earth,
Envy's abhorrèd child, Detraction,
I here expose to thy all-tainting breath
     The issue of my brain: snarl, rail, bark, bite,
     Know that my spirit scorns Detraction's spite.

Know that the Genius, which attendeth on
And guides my powers intellectual,
Holds in all vile repute Detraction.
My soul—an essence metaphysical,
 That in the basest sort scorns critic's rage,
 Because he knows his sacred parentage—

My spirit is not puffed up with fat fume
Of slimy ale, nor Bacchus' heating grape.
My mind disdains the dungy muddy scum
Of abject thoughts and Envy's raging hate.
 True judgment slight regards Opinion,
 A sprightly wit disdains Detraction.

A partial praise shall never elevate
My settled censure of my own esteem:
A cankered verdict of malignant hate
Shall ne'er provoke me worse myself to deem.
 Spite of despite and rancour's villany,
 I am myself, so is my poesy.

John Marston

[URIZEN'S CURSE UPON HIS CHILDREN]*

Then Urizen wept & thus his lamentation poured forth

O horrible O dreadful state! those whom I loved best
On whom I pourd the beauties of my light adorning them
With jewels & precious ornament labourd with art divine
Vests of the radiant colours of heaven & crowns of golden fire
I gave sweet lillies to their breasts & roses to their hair
I taught them songs of sweet delight. I gave their tender voices

Into the blue expanse & I invented with laborious art
Sweet instruments of sound. in pride encompassing my Knees
They pourd their radiance above all. the daughters of Luvah Envied
At their exceeding brightness & the sons of eternity sent them gifts
Now will I pour my fury on them & I will reverse
The precious benediction. for their colours of loveliness

I will give blackness for jewels hoary frost for ornament deformity
For crowns wreathd Serpents for sweet odors stinking corruptibility
For voices of delight hoarse croakings inarticulate thro frost
For labourd fatherly care & sweet instruction. I will give
Chains of dark ignorance & cords of twisted self conceit
And whips of stern repentance & food of stubborn obstinacy
That they may curse Tharmas their God & Los his adopted son
That they may curse & worship the obscure Demon of destruction
That they may worship terrors & obey the violent
Go forth sons of my curse   Go forth daughters of my abhorrence

                    *   *   *   *

For Urizen beheld the terrors of the Abyss wandring among
The ruind spirits once his children & the children of Luvah
Scard at the sound of their own sigh that seems to shake the
        immense
They wander Moping in their heart a Sun a Dreary moon
A Universe of fiery constellations in their brain
An Earth of wintry woe beneath their feet & round their loins
Waters or winds or clouds or brooding lightnings & pestilential
        plagues
Beyond the bounds of their own self their senses cannot penetrate
As the tree knows not what is outside of its leaves & bark
And yet it drinks the summer joy & fears the winter sorrow
So in the regions of the grave none knows his dark compeer
Tho he partakes of his dire woes & mutual returns the pang

The throb the dolor the convulsion in soul sickening woes
The horrid shapes & sights of torment in burning dungeons & in
Fetters of red hot iron some with crowns of serpents & some
With monsters girding round their bosoms. Some lying on beds of
    sulphur
On racks & wheels he beheld women marching oer burning wastes
Of Sand in bands of hundreds & of fifties & of thousands strucken
    with
Lightnings which blazed after them upon their shoulders in their
    march
In successive vollies with loud thunders swift flew the King of Light
Over the burning desarts   Then the desarts passd. involvd in
    clouds
Of smoke with myriads moping in the stifling vapours. Swift
Flew the King tho flagd his powers labring. till over rocks
And Mountains faint weary he wanderd. where multitudes were
    shut
Up in the solid mountains & in rocks which heaved with their
    torments
Then came he among fiery cities & castles built of burning steel
Then he beheld the forms of tygers & of Lions dishumanizd men
Many in serpents & in worms stretchd out enormous length
Over the sullen mould & slimy tracks obstruct his way
Drawn out from deep to deep woven by ribbd
And scaled monsters or armd in iron shell or shell of brass
Or gold a glittering torment shining & hissing in eternal pain
Some [as] columns of fire or of water sometimes stretchd out in
    heighth
Sometimes in length sometimes englobing wandering in vain
    seeking for ease
His voice to them was but an inarticulate thunder for their Ears

Were heavy & dull & their eyes & nostrils closed up
Oft he stood by a howling victim Questioning in words

Soothing or Furious no one answerd every one wrapd up
In his own sorrow howld regardless of his words, nor voice
Of sweet response could he obtain tho oft assayd with tears
He knew they were his Children ruind in his ruind world

William Blake
The Four Zoas

AGAINST EDUCATION

Accurst the man whom Fate ordains in spite—
And cruel parents teach—to read and write!
What need of letters? wherefore should we spell?
Why write our names?—a mark would do as well.
Much are the precious hours of youth misspent
In climbing learning's rugged, steep ascent.
When to the top the bold adventurer's got
He reigns, vain monarch, o'er a barren spot,
Whilst in the vale of ignorance below
Folly and Vice to rank luxuriance grow,
Honours and wealth pour in on every side,
And proud Preferment rolls her golden tide;
O'er crabbèd authors life's gay prime to waste,
To cramp wild genius in the chains of taste,
To bear the slavish drudgery of schools
And tamely stoop to every pedant's rules;
For seven long years debarred of liberal ease,
To plod in college trammels to degrees;
Beneath the weight of solemn toys to groan,
Sleep over books, and leave mankind unknown;
To praise each senior blockhead's threadbare tale
And laugh till freedom blush and spirits fail;
Manhood, with vile submission, to disgrace

And cap the fool whose merit is his place:
Vice-chancellors, whose knowledge is but small,
And chancellors, who nothing know at all.

Charles Churchill

SONNET—TO SCIENCE

Science! true daughter of Old Time thou art!
   Who alterest all things with thy peering eyes.
Why preyest thou thus upon the poet's heart,
   Vulture, whose wings are dull realities?
How should he love thee? or how deem thee wise,
   Who wouldst not leave him in his wandering
To seek for treasure in the jewelled skies,
   Albeit he soared with an undaunted wing?
Hast thou not dragged Diana from her car?
   And driven the Hamadryad from the wood
To seek a shelter in some happier star?
   Hast thou not torn the Naiad from her flood,
The Elfin from the green grass, and from me
The summer dream beneath the tamarind tree?

Edgar Allan Poe

THE GODS OF THE COPYBOOK HEADINGS

1919

As I pass through my incarnations in every age and race,
I make my proper prostrations to the Gods of the Market-Place.
Peering through reverent fingers I watch them flourish and fall,
And the Gods of the Copybook Headings, I notice, outlast them all.

We were living in trees when they met us. They showed us each in
  turn
That Water would certainly wet us, as Fire would certainly burn:
But we found them lacking in Uplift, Vision and Breadth of Mind,
So we left them to teach the Gorillas while we followed the March
  of Mankind.

We moved as the Spirit listed. *They* never altered their pace,
Being neither cloud nor wind-borne like the Gods of the Market-Place;
But they always caught up with our progress, and presently word
  would come
That a tribe had been wiped off its icefield, or the lights had gone
  out in Rome.

With the Hopes that our World is built on they were utterly out of
  touch,
They denied that the Moon was Stilton; they denied she was even
  Dutch.
They denied that Wishes were Horses; they denied that a Pig had
  Wings.
So we worshipped the Gods of the Market Who promised these
  beautiful things.

When the Cambrian measures were forming, They promised
  perpetual peace.
They swore, if we gave them our weapons, that the wars of the
  tribes would cease.
But when we disarmed They sold us and delivered us bound to our
  foe,
And the Gods of the Copybook Headings said: *"Stick to the Devil you
  know."*

On the first Feminian Sandstones we were promised the Fuller Life
(Which started by loving our neighbour and ended by loving his
  wife)

Till our women had no more children and the men lost reason and
faith,
And the Gods of the Copybook Headings said: *"The Wages of Sin is
Death."*

In the Carboniferous Epoch we were promised abundance for all,
By robbing selected Peter to pay for collective Paul;
But, though we had plenty of money, there was nothing our money
could buy,
And the Gods of Copybook Headings said: *"If you don't work you
die."*

Then the Gods of the Market tumbled, and their smooth-tongued
wizards withdrew,
And the hearts of the meanest were humbled and began to believe
it was true
That All is not Gold that Glitters, and Two and Two make Four—
And the Gods of the Copybook Headings limped up to explain it
once more.

.   .   .   .

As it will be in the future, it was at the birth of Man—
There are only four things certain since Social Progress began:—
That the Dog returns to his Vomit and the Sow returns to her Mire,
And the burnt Fool's bandaged finger goes wabbling back to the
Fire;

And that after this is accomplished, and the brave new world begins
When all men are paid for existing and no man must pay for his
sins,
As surely as Water will wet us, as surely as Fire will burn,
The Gods of the Copybook Headings with terror and slaughter
return!

Rudyard Kipling

'A SALESMAN IS AN IT THAT STINKS EXCUSE'

a salesman is an it that stinks Excuse

Me whether it's president of the you were say
or a jennelman name misder finger isn't
important whether it's millions of other punks
or just a handful absolutely doesn't
matter and whether it's in lonjewray

or shrouds is immaterial it stinks

a salesman is an it that stinks to please

but whether to please itself or someone else
makes no more difference than if it sells
hate condoms education snakeoil vac
uumcleaners terror strawberries democ
ra(caveat emptor)cy superfluous hair

or Think We've Met subhuman rights Before

E. E. Cummings

THE BUSINESS LIFE

When someone hangs up, having said
to you, "Don't come around again,"
and you have never heard the phone
banged down with such violence
nor the voice vibrate with such venom,
pick up your receiver gently and dial
again, get the same reply; and dial

again, until he threatens. You will
then get used to it, be sick only
instead of shocked. You will live,
and have a pattern to go by, familiar
to your ear, your senses and your dignity.

David Ignatow

THE FIGURE IN THE CARPET

You can never see him
But he's really wall to wall
Stretches from the bedroom
Underneath the grubby finger
Goes down the circle stair
To the great big frigidaire
And then into the hall
He's hardly there at all
But you know he's really there
Cause he's wall to wall
He's the flat man
He's the figure in the carpet

He always needs a good shampoo
He's got real dirt between his teeth
He's very hairy down his spine
He's real foam rubber underneath
The television never sees him
He's down beside the easy chair
You can reach right down and touch him
Feel his face and sweep his hair
You know he's always there

You can stomp right on his can
He's the flat man
He's the figure in the carpet

You can flick your deadly ash
On his Orient mustache
He'll always take your spittle in
With his silly halfway Persian grin
You can cut him cross him
Beat him up and then emboss him
And lay him down along the hall
He's very marked and so abstract
He's always there yet hardly there
He's very wall to wall
He's the flat man
He's the figure in the carpet

James Camp

BABYLON REVISITED

The gaunt thing
with no organs
creeps along the streets
of Europe, she will
commute, in her feathered bat stomach-gown
with no organs
with sores on her insides
even her head
a vast puschamber
of pus (sy) memories
with no organs
nothing to make babies

she will be the great witch of euro-american legend
who sucked the life
from some unknown nigger
whose name will be known
but whose substance will not ever
not even by him
who is dead in a pile of dopeskin

This bitch killed a friend of mine named Bob Thompson
a black painter, a giant, once, she reduced
to a pitiful imitation faggot
full of American holes and a monkey on his back
slapped airplanes
from the empire state building

May this bitch and her sisters, all of them,
receive my words
in all their orifices like lye mixed with
cocola and alaga syrup

feel this shit, bitches, feel it, now laugh your
hysterectic laughs
while your flesh burns
and your eyes peel to red mud

Amiri Baraka

'IN THE TWENTIETH CENTURY OF MY TRESPASS ON EARTH'

In the Twentieth Century of my trespass on earth,
having exterminated one billion heathens,
heretics, Jews, Moslems, witches, mystical seekers,
black men, Asians, and Christian brothers,

every one of them for his own good,

a whole continent of red men for living in unnatural community
and at the same time having relations with the land,
one billion species of animals for being sub-human,
and ready to take on the bloodthirsty creatures from the other
    planets,
I, Christian man, groan out this testament of my last will.

I give my blood fifty parts polystyrene,
twenty-five parts benzene, twenty-five parts good old gasoline,
to the last bomber pilot aloft, that there shall be one acre
in the dull world where the kissing flower may bloom,
which kisses you so long your bones explode under its lips.

My tongue goes to the Secretary of the Dead
to tell the corpses, "I'm sorry, fellows,
the killing was just one of those things
difficult to pre-visualize—like a cow,
say, getting hit by lightning."

My stomach, which has digested
four hundred treaties giving the Indians
eternal right to their land, I give to the Indians,
I throw in my lungs which have spent four hundred years
sucking in good faith on peace pipes.

My soul I leave to the bee
that he may sting it and die, my brain
to the fly, his back the hysterical green color of slime,
that he may suck on it and die, my flesh to the advertising man,
the anti-prostitute, who loathes human flesh for money.

I assign my crooked backbone

to the dice maker, to chop up into dice,
for casting lots as to who shall see his own blood
on his shirt front and who his brother's,
for the race isn't to the swift but to the crooked.

To the last man surviving on earth
I give my eyelids worn out by fear, to wear
in his long nights of radiation and silence,
so that his eyes can't close, for regret
is like tears seeping through closed eyelids.

I give the emptiness my hand: the pinkie picks no more noses,
slag clings to the black stick of the ring finger,
a bit of flame jets from the tip of the fuck-you finger,
the first finger accuses the heart, which has vanished,
on the thumb stump wisps of smoke ask a ride into the emptiness.

In the Twentieth Century of my nightmare
on earth, I swear on my chromium testicles
to this testament
and last will
of my iron will, my fear of love, my itch for money, and my
    madness.

Galway Kinnell
The Book of Nightmares

THE LAMENTATION OF THE OLD PENSIONER

Although I shelter from the rain
Under a broken tree
My chair was nearest to the fire
In every company

That talked of love or politics,
Ere Time transfigured me.

Though lads are making pikes again
For some conspiracy,
And crazy rascals rage their fill
At human tyranny,
My contemplations are of Time
That has transfigured me.

There's not a woman turns her face
Upon a broken tree,
And yet the beauties that I loved
Are in my memory;
I spit into the face of Time
That has transfigured me.

William Butler Yeats

SEND NO MONEY

Standing under the fobbed
Impendent belly of Time
Tell me the truth, I said,
Teach me the way things go.
All the other lads there
Were itching to have a bash,
But I thought wanting unfair:
It and finding out clash.

So he patted my head, booming *Boy,*
There's no green in your eye:
Sit here, and watch the hail

Of occurrence clobber life out
To a shape no one sees—
Dare you look at that straight?
Oh thank you, I said, *Oh yes please,*
And sat down to wait.

Half life is over now,
And I meet full face on dark mornings
The bestial visor, bent in
By the blows of what happened to happen.
What does it prove? Sod all.
In this way I spent youth,
Tracing the trite untransferable
Truss-advertisement, truth.

Philip Larkin

X.

THIS
VILE CREATED
WORLD

There is no spark of reason i' the world,
And all is raked in ashy heaps of beastliness.
JOHN MARSTON, *The Malcontent*

We for a certainty are not the first
  Have sat in taverns while the tempest hurled
Their hopeful plans to emptiness, and cursed
  Whatever brute and blackguard made the world.
A. E. HOUSMAN, 'The chestnut casts his flambeaux'

This is not what man hates,
Yet he can curse but this.
Harsh Gods and hostile Fates
Are dreams! this only *is*—
MATTHEW ARNOLD, "Empedocles on Etna"

[LEAR'S SPEECH TO THE STORM]

Blow, winds, and crack your cheeks! rage! blow!
You cataracts and hurricanoes, spout
Till you have drenched our steeples, drowned the cocks!
You sulfurous and thought-executing fires,
Vaunt-couriers to oak-cleaving thunderbolts,
Singe my white head! And thou, all-shaking thunder,
Smite flat the thick rotundity o' the world!
Crack nature's molds, all germins spill at once
That make ingrateful man!

William Shakespeare
King Lear, III, ii

ANCIENT MUSIC*

Winter is icummen in,
Lhude sing Goddamm,
Raineth drop and staineth slop,
And how the wind doth ramm!
     Sing: Goddamm.
Skiddeth bus and sloppeth us,
An ague hath my ham.
Freezeth river, turneth liver,
     Damn you, sing: Goddamm.
Goddamm, Goddamm, 'tis why I am, Goddamm,
     So 'gainst the winter's balm.
Sing goddamm, damm, sing Goddamm,
Sing goddamm, sing goddamm, DAMM.

Ezra Pound

ON A COCK AT ROCHESTER

Thou cursèd cock, with thy perpetual noise,
May'st thou be capon made, and lose thy voice,
Or on a dunghill may'st thou spend thy blood,
And vermin prey upon thy craven brood;
May rivals tread thy hens before thy face,
Then with redoubled courage give thee chase;
May'st thou be punished for St Peter's crime,
And on Shrove-Tuesday perish in thy prime;
May thy bruised carcass be some beggar's feast—
Thou first and worst disturber of man's rest.

Sir Charles Sedley

MIRIAM TAZEWELL

When Miriam Tazewell heard the tempest bursting
And his wrathy whips across the sky drawn crackling
She stuffed her ears for fright like a young thing
And with heart full of the flowers took to weeping.

But the earth shook dry his old back in good season,
He had weathered storms that drenched him deep as this
    one,
And the sun, Miriam, ascended to his dominion,
The storm was withered against his empyrean.

After the storm she went forth with skirts kilted
To see in the hot sun her lawn deflowered,
Her tulip, iris, peony strung and pelted,
Pots of geranium spilled and the stalks naked.

The spring transpired in that year with no flowers
But the regular stars went busily on their courses,
Suppers and cards were calendared, and some bridals,
And the birds demurely sang in the bitten poplars.

To Miriam Tazewell the whole world was villain,
The principle of the beast was low and masculine,
And not to unstop her own storm and be maudlin,
For weeks she went untidy, she went sullen.

John Crowe Ransom

THE FLY

O hideous little bat, the size of snot,
With polyhedral eye and shabby clothes,
To populate the stinking cat you walk
The promontory of the dead man's nose,
Climb with the fine leg of a Duncan-Phyfe
    The smoking mountains of my food
        And in a comic mood
    In mid-air take to bed a wife.

Riding and riding with your filth of hair
On gluey foot or wing, forever coy,
Hot from the compost and green sweet decay,
Sounding your buzzer like an urchin toy—
You dot all whiteness with diminutive stool,
    In the tight belly of the dead
        Burrow with hungry head
    And inlay maggots like a jewel.

At your approach the great horse stomps and paws
Bringing the hurricane of his heavy tail;
Shod in disease you dare to kiss my hand
Which sweeps against you like an angry flail;
Still you return, return, trusting your wing
    To draw you from the hunter's reach
        That learns to kill to teach
    Disorder to the tinier thing.

My peace is your disaster. For your death
Children like spiders cup their pretty hands
And wives resort to chemistry of war.
In fens of sticky paper and quicksands
You glue yourself to death. Where you are stuck
    You struggle hideously and beg,
        You amputate your leg
    Imbedded in the amber muck.

But I, a man, must swat you with my hate,
Slap you across the air and crush your flight,
Must mangle with my shoe and smear your blood,
Expose your little guts pasty and white,
Knock your head sidewise like a drunkard's hat,
    Pin your wings under like a crow's,
        Tear off your flimsy clothes
    And beat you as one beats a rat.

Then like Gargantua I stride among
The corpses strewn like raisins in the dust,
The broken bodies of the narrow dead
That catch the throat with fingers of disgust.
I sweep. One gyrates like a top and falls
    And stunned, stone blind, and deaf
        Buzzes its frightful F
    And dies between three cannibals.

Karl Shapiro

TO A FINE YOUNG WOMAN,

who being asked by her lover, *Why she kept so filthy a thing as a Snake in her Bosom*; answered, *'Twas to keep a filthier thing out of it, his Hand*; and, *that her Snake was to play with, and cool her in hot Weather*; which was his Aversion.

You with that creeping, twining thing can play,
Yet me, who would crawl o'er you night and day,
And cool you too, you shake off, cast away;
When I would twist myself about you, you
Will squall out, and will from me fling, or throw;
Thy humour thou from Grandam Eve doth take,
To ruin man, art tempted by a snake,
Thy twining serpent, but to hinder me
Of Paradise—that is, enjoying thee—
Who should esteem myself for ever blest
Had I a place, but like him, in thy breast.
Your snake's the devil, a very Satan who
Of Heav'nly bliss deprives both me and you;
Is thy legs' shackles, to keep them from me,
To make thy hands, and thy legs too, less free
When they, I, you too, should the loser be;
Does, to prevent my touching thy hand, twist
Itself about thy tempting arm or wrist.
You seem a very Fury, with your snake
To frighten man from pleasure he would take,
Whilst my aversion you your pleasure make:
You hold your snake fast; me, your worm, let go;
You cry 'tis cool, and I believe it so;
It chills my blood to see't crawl over you,
But if a wriggling worm temptation be,
O Eve's true daughter! (as it is, I see)
To play with then, to cool, divertise thee;
Of one of my presenting be not shy
To handle and to play with constantly,

Which better, sure, will please thee—cool thee, too—
If you'll but handle it, as that you do,
And let it, where it will, about you go,
Which you may find a better creeping thing;
Will tamer grow, too, for your handling,
Please you more if it in your lap you take
And place for it would in your bosom make.
Once play with that worm, you will quit your snake,
Then with thy snake not such a Fury be
Me to keep at more distance still with thee.
I hate that creeping serpent, still possessed
Of either Paradise, thy lap or breast,
Whilst I'm deprived of either dear blest place
By that snake, as of *his* Old Adam was:
He, as a hisser, is a foe to me;
Such, as a rhymer, I will to him be
Who keeps me from enjoying here all bliss,
Thy love, but my sole earthly Paradise,
Till that thy charming and alluring love
Does but my curse from thy temptation prove
By thy damned snake, which does about thee crawl
In reach of my bliss, to beget my fall.

William Wycherley

THE MALDIVE SHARK

About the Shark, phlegmatical one,
Pale sot of the Maldive sea,
The sleek little pilot-fish, azure and slim,
How alert in attendance be.

From his saw-pit of mouth, from his charnel of maw
They have nothing of harm to dread,
But liquidly glide on his ghastly flank
Or before his Gorgonian head;
Or lurk in the port of serrated teeth
In white triple tiers of glittering gates,
And there find a haven when peril's abroad,
An asylum in jaws of the Fates!
They are friends; and friendly they guide him to prey,
Yet never partake of the treat—
Eyes and brains to the dotard lethargic and dull,
Pale ravener of horrible meat.

Herman Melville

THE CROW

The crow in the cage in the dining-room
hates me, because I will not feed him.

And I have left nothing behind in leaving
because I killed him.

And because I hit him over the head with a stick
there is nothing I laugh at.

Sickness is the hatred of a repentance
knowing there is nothing he wants.

Robert Creeley

ON SHOOTING PARTICLES BEYOND THE WORLD

"White Sands, N.M. Dec. 18 (UP) 'We first throw a little something into
the skies,' Zwicky said. 'Then a little more, then a shipload of
instruments—then ourselves.'"

On this day man's disgust is known
Incipient before but now full blown
With minor wars of major consequence,
Duly building empirical delusions.

Now this little creature in a rage
Like new-born infant screaming compleat angler
Objects to the whole globe itself
And with a vicious lunge he throws

Metal particles beyond the orbit of mankind.
Beethoven shaking his fist at death,
A giant dignity in human terms,
Is nothing to this imbecile metal fury.

The world is too much for him. The green
Of earth is not enough, love's deities,
Peaceful intercourse, happiness of nations,
The wild animal dazzled on the desert.

If the maniac would only realize
The comforts of his padded cell
He would have penetrated the
Impenetrability of the spiritual.

It is not intelligent to go too far.
How he frets that he can't go too!
But his particles would maim a star,
His free-floating bombards rock the moon.

Good Boy! We pat the baby to eructate,
We pat him then for eructation.
Good Boy Man! Your innards are put out,
From now all space will be your vomitorium.

The atom bomb accepted this world,
Its hatred of man blew death in his face.
But not content, he'll send slugs beyond,
His particles of intellect will spit on the sun.

Not God he'll catch, in the mystery of space.
He flaunts his own out-cast state
As he throws his imperfections outward bound,
And his shout that gives a hissing sound.

Richard Eberhart

THE CURSE

Hell is a red barn on a hill
With another hill behind the barn
Of dung. The road is stones and dust
And in the road are harpy-hens,
A hound, bones of cattle, flies.

Suddenly on Sunday morning
Out of the dew and stillness, a voice
Out of the barn God-damning cows
At milking. Whoever passes shivers
In the sun and hurries on.

Robert Francis

AL CAPONE IN ALASKA

or hoodoo ecology vs the
judeo-christian tendency to
let em have it!

The Eskimo hunts
the whale & each year
the whale flowers for the
Eskimo.
This must be love baby!
One receiving with respect
from a Giver who has
plenty.
There is no hatred here.
There is One Big Happy
Family here.

American & Canadian Christians
submachine gun the whales.
They gallantly sail out &
shoot them as if the Pacific
were a Chicago garage on
St. Valentine's day.

Ishmael Reed

DR. JOSEPH GOEBBELS

22 April, 1945.

*(On this date, Goebbels moved into the lowest level of the bunker,
taking a room opposite Hitler's.)*

Stand back, make way, you mindless scum,
Squire Voland the Seducer's come—
Old Bock from Babelsberg whose tower
Falls silent now, whose shrunken power

For lies or lays comes hobbling home
Into this concrete catacomb.

Here's Runty Joe, the cunt collector
Who grew to greatness, first erector
Of myths and missions, fibs and fables,
Who pulled the wool then turned the tables;
He piped the tunes and called the dance
Where shirtless countries lost their pants.

Goatfooted Pan, the nation's gander
To whom Pan-Germans all played pander,
The jovial cob-swan quick to cover
Lida Baarova, his check-list lover;
Swellfoot the Tyrant, he could riddle
Men's minds away, hi-diddle-diddle.

Our little Doctor, Joe the Gimp
Comes back to limpness and his limp;
Hephaistos, Vulcan the lame smith
Whose net of lies caught one true myth.
His wife, the famous beauty, whored
By numbskull Mars, the dull warlord.

What if I took my little fling
At conquest, at adventuring,
Pried the lid of Pandora's box off—
There's nothing there to bring your rocks off.
I never saw one fucking day
So fine I courted it to stay.

If I got snarled in my own mesh
Of thighs and bellies, who wants flesh?
I never hankered after matter.
Let Hermann swell up, grosser, fatter,

Weighed down by medals, houses, clothing;
They leave me lean, secured in loathing.

As a young man, I pricked the bubble
Of every creed; I saw that rubble
And offered myself the realms of earth
Just to say Yes. But what's it worth?
No thank you, Ma'am. Behold the Ram
Of God: I doubt, therefore I am.

Here I forsake that long pricktease
Of histories, hopes, lusts, luxuries.
I come back to my first Ideal—
The vacancy that's always real.
I sniffed out all life's openings:
I loved only the holes in things

So strip down one bare cell for this
Lay Brother of the last abyss.
To me, still, all abstractions smell:
My head and nose clear in this cell
Of concrete, this confession booth
Where liars face up to blank truth.

My tongue lashed millions to the knife;
Here, I'll hold hands with my soiled wife.
My lies piped men out, hot to slaughter;
Here, I'll read stories to my daughter
Then hack off all relations, choose
Only the Nothing you can't lose,

Send back this body, fixed in its
Infantile paralysis.
I was born small; I shall grow less

Till I burst into Nothingness,
That slot in time where only pure
Spirit extends, absent and sure.

I am that spirit that denies,
High Priest of Laymen, Prince of Lies.
Your house is founded on my rock;
Truth crows; now I deny my cock.
Jock of this walk, I turn down all,
Robbing my Peter to play Paul.

I give up all goods I possess
To build my faith on faithlessness.
Black Peter, I belie my Lord—
You've got to die to spread the Word.
Now the last act; there's no sequel.
Soon, once more, all things shall be equal.

W. D. Snodgrass
The Führer Bunker

OLD WITHERINGTON

Old Witherington had drunk too much again.
The children changed their play and packed around him
To jeer his latest brawl. Their parents followed.

Prune-black, with bloodshot eyes and one white tooth,
He tottered in the night with legs spread wide
Waving a hatchet. 'Come on, come on,' he piped,
'And I'll baptize these bricks with bloody kindling.
I may be old and drunk, but not afraid
To die. I've died before. A million times

I've died and gone to hell. I live in hell.
If I die now I die, and put an end
To all this loneliness. Nobody cares
Enough to even fight me now, except
This crazy bastard here.'
                          And with these words
He cursed the little children, cursed his neighbors,
Cursed his father, mother, and his wife,
Himself, and God, and all the rest of the world,
All but his grinning adversary, who, crouched,
Danced tenderly around him with a jag-toothed bottle,
As if the world compressed to one old man
Who was the sun, and he sole faithful planet.

Dudley Randall

XI.

SELF‑LOATHING

Which way I fly is Hell; my self am Hell;
And in the lowest deep a lower deep
Still threat'ning to devour me opens wide,
To which the Hell I suffer seems a Heav'n.
SATAN in John Milton's *Paradise Lost*

i
began
to love
only a
part of
me—
my inner
self which
is all
black—
&
developed a
vehement
hatred of
my light
brown
outer.
DON L. LEE,
"The Self-Hatred of Don L. Lee"

A HAND-MIRROR

Hold it up sternly—see this it sends back, (who is it? is it you?)
Outside fair costume, within ashes and filth,
No more a flashing eye, no more a sonorous voice or springy step,
Now some slave's eye, voice, hands, step,
A drunkard's breath, unwholesome eater's face, venerealee's flesh,
Lungs rotting away piecemeal, stomach sour and cankerous,
Joints rheumatic, bowels clogged with abomination,
Blood circulating dark and poisonous streams,
Words babble, hearing and touch callous,
No brain, no heart left, no magnetism of sex;
Such from one look in this looking-glass ere you go hence,
Such a result so soon—and from such a beginning!

Walt Whitman

[LINES WRITTEN DURING A PERIOD OF INSANITY]*

Hatred and vengeance, my eternal portion,
Scarce can endure delay of execution,
Wait with impatient readiness to seize my
                         Soul in a moment.

Damned below Judas: more abhorred than he was,
Who for a few pence sold his holy Master.
Twice-betrayed Jesus me, the last delinquent,
                         Deems the profanest.

Man disavows, and Deity disowns me:
Hell might afford my miseries a shelter;
Therefore Hell keeps her ever-hungry mouths all
                         Bolted against me.

Hard lot! encompassed with a thousand dangers;
Weary, faint, trembling with a thousand terrors;
I'm called, if vanquished, to receive a sentence
                                        Worse than Abiram's.

Him the vindictive rod of angry justice
Sent quick and howling to the center headlong;
I, fed with judgment, in a fleshly tomb, am
                                        Buried above ground.

William Cowper

'I AM THE ONLY BEING WHOSE DOOM'

I am the only being whose doom
No tongue would ask, no eye would mourn;
I never caused a thought of gloom,
A smile of joy, since I was born.

In secret pleasure, secret tears,
This changeful life has slipped away,
As friendless after eighteen years,
As lone as on my natal day.

There have been times I cannot hide,
There have been times when this was drear,
When my sad soul forgot its pride
And longed for one to love me here.

But those were in the early glow
Of feelings since subdued by care;
And they have died so long ago,

I hardly now believe they were.

First melted off the hope of youth,
Then fancy's rainbow fast withdrew;
And then experience told me truth
In mortal bosoms never grew.

'Twas grief enough to think mankind
All hollow, servile, insincere;
But worse to trust to my own mind
And find the same corruption there.

Emily Brontë

'I WAKE AND FEEL THE FELL OF DARK, NOT DAY'

I wake and feel the fell of dark, not day.
What hours, O what black hoûrs we have spent
This night! what sights you, heart, saw; ways you went!
And more must, in yet longer light's delay.
    With witness I speak this. But where I say
Hours I mean years, mean life. And my lament
Is cries countless, cries like dead letters sent
To dearest him that lives alas! away.
    I am gall, I am heartburn. God's most deep decree
Bitter would have me taste: my taste was me;
Bones built in me, flesh filled, blood brimmed the curse.
    Selfyeast of spirit a dull dough sours. I see
The lost are like this, and their scourge to be
As I am mine, their sweating selves; but worse.

Gerard Manley Hopkins

THE OCTOPUS

A shameless thing, for ilka vileness able,
It is deid grey as dust, the dust o' a man.
I perish o' a nearness I canna win awa' frae,
Its deidly coils aboot my buik are thrawn.

A shaggy poulp, embracin' me and stingin',
And as a serpent cauld agen' my hert.
Its scales are poisoned shafts that jag me to the quick
—And waur than them's my scunner's fearfu' smert!

O that its prickles were a knife indeed,
But it is thowless, flabby, dowf, and numb.
Sae sluggishly it drains my benmaist life
A dozent dragon, dreidfu', deef, and dumb.

In mum obscurity it twines its obstinate rings
And hings caressin'ly, its purpose whole;
And this deid thing, whale-white obscenity,
This horror that I writhe in—is my soul!

Hugh MacDiarmid

HUMAN RELATIONS

My mind is so evil and unjust
I smile in deprecation when I am flattered
But inside the palace of my smile
Is the grovelling worm that eats its own tail
And concealed under the threshold of my lips
Is the trustless word that will wrong you if it can.

Come nearer to me therefore, my friend,
And be impressed by the truth of my explanation.
No less, lady, take my chaste hand
While the other imaginatively rifles your drawers.

C. H. Sisson

INTERVIEW WITH DOCTOR DRINK

I have a fifth of therapy
In the house, and transference there.
Doctor, there's not much wrong with me,
Only a sick rattlesnake somewhere

In the house, if it be there at all,
But the lithe mouth is coiled. The shapes
Of door and window move. I call.
What is it that pulls down the drapes,

Disheveled and exposed? Your rye
Twists in my throat: intimacy
Is like hard liquor. Who but I
Coil there and squat, and pay your fee?

J. V. Cunningham

THE COST OF PRETENDING

I would despise myself if I had the strength for it,
Would welcome the knife slitting the skin of my neck
As long as it did not falter and pour the blood.

Give me your hand, put it beneath my arm
Which closes on it, next to my heart. What
Do you hear of me? A steady beat, dull, leaden,
Irreversible. One who survives everything
Will shortly survive even himself.

Peter Davison

LATE-FLOWERING LUST

My head is bald, my breath is bad.
    Unshaven is my chin,
I have not now the joys I had
    When I was young in sin.

I run my fingers down your dress
    With brandy-certain aim
And you respond to my caress
    And maybe feel the same.

But I've a picture of my own
    On this reunion night,
Wherein two skeletons are shewn
    To hold each other tight;

Dark sockets look on emptiness
    Which once was loving-eyed,
The mouth that opens for a kiss
    Has got no tongue inside.

I cling to you inflamed with fear
    As now you cling to me,
I feel how frail you are my dear

And wonder what will be—

A week? or twenty years remain?
    And then—what kind of death?
A losing fight with frightful pain
    Or a gasping fight for breath?

Too long we let our bodies cling,
    We cannot hide disgust
At all the thoughts that in us spring
    From this late-flowering lust.

John Betjeman

EPIDERMAL MACABRE

Indelicate is he who loathes
The aspect of his fleshy clothes,—
The flying fabric stitched on bone,
The vesture of the skeleton,
The garment neither fur nor hair,
The cloak of evil and despair,
The veil long violated by
Caresses of the hand and eye.
Yet such is my unseemliness:
I hate my epidermal dress,
The savage blood's obscenity,
The rags of my anatomy,
And willingly would I dispense
With false accouterments of sense,
To sleep immodestly, a most
Incarnadine and carnal ghost.

Theodore Roethke

TO A BAD HEART

Speak, thou jaded heart, defective heart,
heart kneaded with cold water, scraggy heart,
short-winded heart, devourous heart, hooked heart,
ass-ridden, over-lechered, plucked-up heart,
bestunk, maleficated, lumpish, prolix
heart, heart, heart, beblistered, seedless, void:
What will you promise now? Last time you swore—
remember? in the barn?—things would be different;
but nothing's ever different. And I'm fed up.
Get out! This time I swear I'm serious. Heart,
I've longed to see you dead. I've dreamed of you
cold as a cow's heart in a butcher's showcase
jutting your battleship big guns, a beef-chunk
blood-drained, koshered, pure. I tell you, heart,
you World's Most Perfectly Developed Heart,
bottlecap-bender unable to touch your ear,
armpit-razored oiled bronze bulging hulk,
those flabby fairy hearts that whistle at you
are such as kick chairs in their scrawny rage,
frustrated, pimply, adolescent hearts
who know you only on the comic covers
posed like a rock of muscle. Oh, I have seen you,
heart, yes you, you Cardiac Giant, cringe
before a simple heart one-half your size,
solaced you dragging your bruised auricles home,
aorta between your legs like a booted dog,
snivelling of some gang of bullies. Sero
te amavi, tough but O so gentle.
Compare those swollen ventricles with the hard
lissome chambers of any healthy heart,
grown through those flexions natural to hearts
tough and able to take care of itself,

not bloated like a vacuumcleaner-bag
with strained, incessant, unnatural exercise.
You ought to be ashamed, you hear me, heart?
What did I do to deserve a heart like you?

Tim Reynolds

ECZEMA

Tearing at my package like a child
eager for its present, I scratch my back
between the shoulder blades, my arms, my chest,
my face, and bloody myself, like one of those wild
self-flagellating enthusiasts. The attack
subsides eventually. Exhausted, I rest

but know another episode is waiting,
another battle in this civil war
my body wages with itself. My skin
erupts periodically; it's something hating
itself, the spirit revolting at the poor
flesh it must inhabit, is trapped within.

Doctors call it a psychogenic condition,
like asthma or colitis; it is an ill
in which the skin's itch is the soul's fret,
and scratching is the body's act of contrition.
I try to absolve with an antihistamine pill
and not to get excited, not to sweat,

but there is a rage inside me, a prophet's deep

revulsion at the flesh. When it gets bad,
I scratch as in a dream of purity,
of bare-boned whiteness, clean enough to keep
the soul that's mired there now, driving me mad,
desperate, righteous, clawing to be free.

David Slavitt

'GOOD RIDDANCE TO BAD RUBBISH O AT LAST'

Good riddance to bad rubbish O at last
my teeth, for forty years you couldn't crack nuts
nor greedily suck out the sweet juice of corn,
but pain I had from you hundreds of horrible nights
when being poor I couldn't get help
and being puritanical I wouldn't take aspirin.
From the beginning you were misshapen
and a damned baseball broke the best of you
leaving ugly my wasted youth among the Americans
who set great store on regular and flashing teeth.
Now I am rich and an exquisite craftsman
will fashion me a bright smile not my own.
If I had bitten the world angrily,
as it did me, I too might have had vigorous teeth.
But my way is to be patient, and I have survived
even to this year not worse than the last.

Paul Goodman

ONE WRITING AGAINST HIS PRICK

Base metal hanger by your master's thigh!
Eternal shame to all prick's heraldry,
Hide thy despisèd head and do not dare
To peep—no, not so much as take the air

But through a buttonhole, but pine and die
Confined within the codpiece monast'ry.
The little childish boy that hardly knows
The way through which his urine flows,
Touched by my mistress her magnetic hand,
His little needle presently will stand.
Did she not clap her legs about my back,
Her porthole open? Damned prick, what is't you lack?
Henceforth stand stiff and gain your credit lost,
Or I'll ne'er draw thee, but against a post.

Anonymous
English, late seventeenth century

'AND NOW YOU'RE READY WHO WHILE SHE WAS HERE'

And now you're ready who while she was here
Hung like a flag in calm. Friend, though you stand
Erect and eager, in your eye a tear,
I will not pity you, or lend a hand.

J. V. Cunningham

INTRODUCING A MADMAN*

He finished his speech in a
gruesome way. Ha! Ha!

I can feel it wet round
her neck, for now
both mother and daugher lay in it, more
radiantly beautiful than ever.

Introducing a madman: My God!
what has happened to him?

Crush me with fear and
horror, you so
clever lady (with a
strength which seemed incredible).

Keith Waldrop

LOVE THE WILD SWAN

"I hate my verses, every line, every word.
Oh pale and brittle pencils ever to try
One glass-blade's curve, or the throat of one bird
That clings to twig, ruffled against white sky.
Oh cracked and twilight mirrors ever to catch
One color, one glinting flash, of the splendor of things.
Unlucky hunter, Oh bullets of wax,
The lion beauty, the wild-swan wings, the storm of the
    wings."
—This wild swan of a world is no hunter's game.
Better bullets than yours would miss the white breast,
Better mirrors than yours would crack in the flame.
Does it matter whether you hate your . . . self? At
    least
Love your eyes that can see, your mind that can
Hear the music, the thunder of the wings. Love the wild
    swan.

Robinson Jeffers

THE HEART

In the desert
I saw a creature, naked, bestial,
Who, squatting upon the ground,
Held his heart in his hands,
And ate of it.

I said, "Is it good, friend?"
"It is bitter—bitter," he answered;
"But I like it
Because it is bitter,
And because it is my heart."

Stephen Crane

XII.

AGAINST HATE

Done is a battell on the dragon blak . . .

WILLIAM DUNBAR

think of filth, is it really awesome
neither is hate

FRANK O'HARA, "Poem"

Love, thou art absolute sole lord
Of life and death.

RICHARD CRASHAW, "In Memory of the Virtuous
and Learned Lady Madre de Teresa"

SONG

Make this night loveable,
Moon, and with eye single
Looking down from up there
Bless me, One especial,
And friends everywhere.

With a cloudless brightness
Surround our absences;
Innocent by our sleeps,
Watched by great still spaces,
White hills, glittering deeps.

Parted by circumstance,
Grant each your indulgence
That we may meet in dreams
For talk, for dalliance,
By warm hearths, by cool streams.

Shine lest tonight any,
In the dark suddenly,
Wake alone in a bed
To hear his own fury
Wishing his love were dead.

W. H. Auden

'THE PALLID THUNDERSTRICKEN SIGH FOR GAIN'

The pallid thunderstricken sigh for gain,
Down an ideal stream they ever float,
And sailing on Pactolus in a boat,
Drown soul and sense, while wistfully they strain

Weak eyes upon the glistering sands that robe
The understream. The wise, could he behold
Cathedraled caverns of thick-ribbèd gold
And branching silvers of the central globe,
Would marvel from so beautiful a sight
How scorn and ruin, pain and hate could flow:
But Hatred in a gold cave sits below:
Pleached with her hair, in mail of argent light
Shot into gold, a snake her forehead clips,
And skins the colour from her trembling lips.

Alfred, Lord Tennyson

I HATE THAT DRUM'S DISCORDANT SOUND*

I hate that drum's discordant sound,
Parading round, and round, and round:
To thoughtless youth it pleasure yields,
And lures from cities and from fields,
To sell their liberty for charms
Of tawdry lace and glittering arms;
And when Ambition's voice commands,
To march, and fight, and fall, in foreign lands.

I hate that drum's discordant sound,
Parading round, and round, and round:
To me it talks of ravag'd plains,
And burning towns, and ruin'd swains,
And mangled limbs, and dying groans,
And widows' tears, and orphans' moans;
And all that Misery's hand bestows,
To fill the catalogue of human woes.

John Scott

NIGHTMARE INSPECTION TOUR FOR AMERICAN GENERALS

Though you tear the medals
From your chests and pray
Not to go, though you whimper
And shrink in a cold huddle
Of dogs crying *Semper
Fidelis*, I come to say

It is your solemn duty.
You have seen the yellow
Babies bombed back to their
Leaking bones, the whole air
Wild with the fluting
Of their mothers lost in woe,

You have seen the dead shoved
Into their sleeping bags,
The wrecked boys lowered from
The choppers, a left arm
Gone or a shredded leg,
And you have not been moved.

You have seen everything,
You have seen nothing.
I have come to take you
Somewhere out of my mind.
I am not one of you
And yet I am your kind.

I never laid down any
Body's life, but I have
Paid you to, I have laid

Down on the line good money
Made from poetry and love
For you to count the dead.

So I will take you where
We are damned to go,
Through the dreamed hospital,
Ranks of white beds fatal
And blank as graves of snow,
Through the stone bunkers clear

Of everything but cold
Muzzles slanted for the kill,
Down the edge of a field
You will believe you know
Until it suddenly wells
Up with a light so

Fierce we can see nothing
But what we came to see,
Hunched over like burnt stacks
Of entrails under a black
Flap of night like the wing
Of a buried banshee

Angel, hugging their bones
In the cold or clawing
At their chests for medals,
Huddled on the ripples
Of an undug grave, knowing
Their only lives are gone

Far from them in a deep

River of tears beneath
Their blackening deaths,
The dead pride of our own
Mother country, weeping
To be let down.

Gibbons Ruark

THE FURY OF HATING EYES

I would like to bury
all the hating eyes
under the sand somewhere off
the North Atlantic and suffocate
them with the awful sand
and put all their colors to sleep
in that soft smother.
Take the brown eyes of my father,
those gun shots, those mean muds.
Bury them.
Take the blue eyes of my mother,
naked as the sea,
waiting to pull you down
where there is no air, no God.
Bury them.
Take the black eyes of my lover,
coal eyes like a cruel hog,
wanting to whip you and laugh.
Bury them.
Take the hating eyes of martyrs,
presidents, bus collectors,
bank managers, soldiers.

Bury them.
Take my eyes, half blind
and falling into the air.
Bury them.
Take your eyes.
I come to the center,
where a shark looks up at death
and thinks of my death.
They'd like to take my heart
and squeeze it like a doughnut.
They'd like to take my eyes
and poke a hatpin through
their pupils. Not just to bury
but to stab. As for your eyes,
I fold up in front of them
in a baby ball and you send
them to the State Asylum.
Look! Look! Both those
mice are watching you
from behind the kind bars.

Anne Sexton

HATRED OF MEN WITH BLACK HAIR

I hear voices praising Tshombe, and the Portuguese
In Angola, these are the men who skinned Little Crow!
We are all their sons, skulking
In back rooms, selling nails with trembling hands!

We distrust every person on earth with black hair;
We send teams to overthrow Chief Joseph's government;
We train natives to kill Presidents with blowdarts;

We have men loosening the nails on Noah's ark.

The State Department floats in the heavy jellies near the bottom
Like exhausted crustaceans, like squids who are confused,
Sending out beams of black light to the open sea,
Fighting their fraternal feeling for the great landlords.

We have violet rays that light up the jungles at night, showing
The friendly populations; we are teaching the children of ritual
To overcome their longing for life, and we send
Sparks of black light that fit the holes in the generals' eyes.

Underneath all the cement of the Pentagon
There is a drop of Indian blood preserved in snow:
Preserved from a trail of blood that once led away
From the stockade, over the snow, the trail now lost.

Robert Bly

HOW TO CHANGE THE U.S.A.

From an interview New York Times, *May 12, 1968*

For openers, the Federal Government
    the honkies, the pigs in blue
must go down South
    and take those crackers out of bed,
the crackers who blew up
    those four little girls
in that Birmingham church,
    those crackers who murdered
Medgar Evars and killed
    the three civil rights workers—

they must pull them out of bed
    and kill them with axes
in the middle of the street.
    Chop them up with dull axes.
      Slowly.
At high noon.
    With everybody watching
on television.
    Just as a gesture
of good faith.

Harry Edwards
arranged into verse form by Walter Lowenfels

FIRST PRACTICE

After the doctor checked to see
we weren't ruptured,
the man with the short cigar took us
under the grade school,
where we went in case of attack
or storm, and said
he was Clifford Hill, he was
a man who believed dogs
ate dogs, he had once killed
for his country, and if
there were any girls present
for them to leave now.
    No one
left. OK, he said, he said I take
that to mean you are hungry
men who hate to lose as much
as I do. OK. Then

he made two lines of us
facing each other,
and across the way, he said,
is the man you hate most
in the world,
and if we are to win
that title I want to see how.
But I don't want to see
any marks when you're dressed,
he said. He said, *Now.*

Gary Gildner

HYMN TO DISPEL HATRED AT MIDNIGHT

Here where I watch the dew
That gathers by the door,
Here where the time is true
    And on the floor
My shadow stirs no more,

The slow night burns away.
Nay, neither I nor Time
Can manage quite to stay—
    We seek a clime
Bound in a moment's chime.

Men are like blades of grass
Beneath a winter sky,
The constellations pass,
    The air is dry
From star to living eye.

Hence unto God, unsought,
My anguish sets. Oh, vain
The heart that hates! Oh, naught
   So drenched in pain!
Grief will not turn again.

Yvor Winters

IN THE OLD GUERILLA WAR

In the old guerilla war
between father and son
I am the no man's land.
When the moon shows
over my scorched breast
they fire across me.
If a bullet ricochets
and I bleed,
they say it is my time
of month.
Sometimes I iron
handkerchiefs
into flags of truce,
hide them in pockets;
or humming, I roll socks
instead of bandages.
Then we sit down together
breaking only bread.
The family tree
shades us, the snipers
waiting in its branches
sleep between green leaves.
I think of the elm

sending its roots
like spies underground
through any rough terrain
in search of water;
or Noah sending out the dove
to find land.
Only survive long enough;
the triggers
will rust into rings
around both their fingers.
I will be a field
where all the flowers
on my housedress
bloom at once.

Linda Pastan

THE GOOD MAN IN HELL

If a good man were ever housed in Hell
   By needful error of the qualities,
Perhaps to prove the rule or shame the devil,
   Or speak the truth only a stranger sees,

Would he, surrendering quick to obvious hate,
   Fill half eternity with cries and tears,
Or watch beside Hell's little wicket gate
   In patience for the first ten thousand years,

Feeling the curse climb slowly to his throat
   That, uttered, dooms him to rescindless ill,
Forcing his praying tongue to run by rote,
   Eternity entire before him still?

Would he at last, grown faithful in his station,
  Kindle a little hope in hopeless Hell,
And sow among the damned doubts of damnation,
  Since here someone could live and could live well?

One doubt of evil would bring down such a grace,
  Open such a gate, all Eden could enter in,
Hell be a place like any other place,
  And love and hate and life and death begin.

Edwin Muir

NOTES

Page 11. *'This book is one thing, / Christ's curse is another.'* For a bookplate that might make a thief think twice, these lines, in different versions, commonly served. Sources are given by Carleton Brown and R. H. Robbins, *Index of Middle English Verse* (New York: Columbia University Press, 1943), no. 3580.

Page 25. *Ribh Considers Christian Love Insufficient.* The fifth of twelve "Supernatural Songs," probably written in 1934. Ribh, Yeats noted, is an "old hermit" whose Christianity antedates Saint Patrick and hence "echoes pre-Christian thought." The poem appears to have grown out of some automatic writing: Mrs. Yeats had been taking down the thoughts of a spirit who told Yeats, "'hate God,' we must hate all ideas concerning God that we possess, that if we did not, absorption in God would be impossible" (Yeats's journal quoted by Richard Ellmann, *The Identity of Yeats*, New York: Oxford University Press, 1964, p. 283).

Page 30. *The White City.* No doubt the city is New York, where McKay had come from his native Jamaica. He first published this poem in 1921 in the *Liberator*, a revolutionary political journal he helped edit.

Page 39. *Inheritance.* Like "Love and Hate" in the preceding section, "Inheritance" is a translation from the Irish. O'Connor believed it to be a medieval interpretation of a text from Ecclesiastes: "And what is the new kingdom [man] inherits? Creeping things and carrion beast, and worm."

Page 40. *Daddy.* The poet's father, Otto Plath, was born a German citizen in Grabow, a town in the Polish corridor. He died in Boston in 1940, when the poet was eight, following the amputation of a gangrened leg. He was neither a bundist nor a Hitler sympathizer. "Despite everything," A. Alvarez has remarked, "'Daddy' is a love poem."

Page 58. *The Brockton Murder.* This Massachusetts murder case is detailed by William James in *The Dilemma of Determinism*.

Page 64. *Upon Scobble.* Herrick as vicar may have been observing behavior in his congregation. According to L. C. Martin, there are several Scobbles or Scobells in the register of Dean Prior Parish. The poet's "Discontents in Devon" suggests that he wrote in order to enliven his time:

> More discontents I never had
>   Since I was born than here,
> Where I have been, and still am, sad
>   In this dull Devonshire.
> Yet justly too I must confess
>   I ne'er invented such
> Ennobled numbers for the press
>   Than where I loathed so much.

Page 73. *The Lady's-Maid's Song.* Hollander wrote this song for a production of George Etherege's *The Man of Mode* staged at Barnard College in 1951.

Page 75. *'I do not like thee, Doctor Fell.'* These lines have often been claimed by Mother Goose. According to tradition, this impromptu translation saved Brown from expulsion from Christ Church. Dr. Fell, dean of the college, offered to stay Brown's punishment if the young satirist could put into English the epigram of Martial:

> Non amo te, Sabidi, nec possum dicere quare;
> Hoc tantum possum dicere, Non amo te.

Page 78. *A Song.* Sung in Edward Ravenscroft's play *The Canterbury Guests* (1694), to music by Henry Purcell. This text, slightly edited, is from Thomas D'Urfey's *Wit and Mirth, or, Pills to Purge Melancholy*, vol. 5 (London, 1719–20).

Page 80. *'When Sir Joshua Reynolds died.'* Blake wrote these lines in his copy of *The Works of Sir Joshua Reynolds*, next to an account of the painter's death in 1792, due to the "inordinate growth" of his liver.

Page 83. *Black Bull of Aldgate.* The coach to Epping Forest, where Tennyson made his home from 1837 to 1840, took on passengers in front of this London inn. The pun in the last line refers to the bull published by Pope Clement VII condemning the marriage of Henry VIII to Anne Boleyn.

Page 84. *I Wish My Tongue Were A Quiver.* This seething lyric first appeared in a collection called *Viper's Bugloss* (Toronto: Ryerson Press, 1938), under the pen name John Smalacombe. MacKay has also written a study, *The Wrath of Homer* (Toronto: University of Toronto Press, 1948).

Page 85. *Skin the Goat's Curse on Carey.* The text of this broadside ballad, first printed and sold in Dublin in 1883, is taken from Georges-Denis Zimmermann's *Songs of Irish Rebellion* (Hatboro, Pa.: Folklore Associates, 1967). James Fitzharris, popularly dubbed Skin the Goat, was the cabman sentenced to prison for driving the assassins of Thomas Burke and Lord Cavendish to Phoenix Park. James Carey was the informer who helped obtain Fitzharris's conviction. Set free seventeen years later, Skin the Goat returned to Dublin, where he kept a cabman's shelter. James Joyce makes him a character in *Ulysses*.

Page 89. *A Glass of Beer.* Curses of this kind may well have been in the air in the pubs of Stephens's native Dublin. Padraic Colum, in *An Anthology of Irish Verse* (New York: Liveright, 1948), notes that this poem is a translation from the Irish of David O'Bruaidar.

Page 90. *Gas from a Burner.* In 1912, after his Irish publisher George Roberts of Maunsel and Company had broken an agreement to publish *Dubliners*, Joyce had this ironic monologue printed in Trieste as a broadside, and sent copies to his brother Charles to be given away in Dublin. Figures of the Irish literary renaissance are mentioned: George Moore, James Cousins, J. M. Synge, Padraic Colum. "Mountainy Mutton" is the poet Joseph Campbell;

"Gregory of the Golden Mouth," Lady Gregory. Before turning publisher, Roberts had been a commercial traveller for a manufacturer of ladies' undergarments; and "Maunsel's manager's travelling bag" figures in an anecdote recorded by Joyce's younger brother, Stanislaus. One afternoon, paying an unannounced call on the Dublin headquarters of the Hermetic Society, James Joyce and Oliver St. John Gogarty found the rooms empty, except for member Roberts's bag of underwear samples. Later, arriving in the company of a Miss Mitchell, George Russell (AE), master of the society, was displeased to be greeted by a pair of drawers strung between two chairs, with "the handle of the Hermetic broom between the legs" (Stanislaus Joyce, *My Brother's Keeper*, New York: Viking, 1958, pp. 254–55).

Page 103. *If Justice Moved.* Bettie M. Sellers has provided this account of how the poem came to her: "Treachery of the basest order was done to one of mine—I tried to write it and the paper kept charring. Deciding that the anger was too hot, I put away the hurt, hoping to forget it. Then, one evening some six months later, I was watching the news—there was a mother whose small son had been murdered. In the strange way that poetry has of putting disparate things together, I was able to wear that mother's mask and gain enough objectivity to write my own anger without burning up the paper. Of course, my teacher-of-literature self was there as well, since at the time I was involved in the teaching of Dante's *Inferno*. I am not sure that I understand how the mask works, but often it does enable me to speak of things that otherwise I could not handle." The poet is a professor in the Humanities Division of Young Harris College.

Page 109. *The Blacksmiths.* Wesli Court has preserved much of the rhythm and alliterative music of his original, from the fifteenth-century Arundel manuscript (3227 in the *Index of Middle English Verse*). The first ten lines will give a sense of it:

> Swarte-smeked smethes, smatered with smoke,
> Drive me to deth with den of here dintes:
> Swich nois on nightes ne herd men never,
> What knavene cry and clatering of knockes!
> The cammede kongons cryen after "Col! col!"
> And blowen here bellewes that all here brain brestes.
> "Huf, puf," seith that on, "Haf, paf," that other.
> They spitten and sprawlen and spellen many spelles,
> They gnawen and gnacchen, they grones togidere,
> And holden hem hote with here hard hamers.

Page 110. *[An Execration against Whores].* Webster places this speech in the mouth of Monticelso, a cardinal, afterward Pope Paul IV. What tribute was paid in the Low Countries "even on man's perdition"? Apparently, in Holland at the time, a tax on fornication was levied.

Page 111. Sonnet 18. Milton sees the Waldenses as true primitive Christians. They had broken with Rome in the twelfth century, refusing to accept dogmas and rituals that, they believed, had been added too recently. In January 1655, Immanuel, Duke of Savoy, decreed that their descendants, the Vaudois, must either convert to Roman Catholicism or quit their Piemont homes. They resisted, and in April were massacred by a motley army of French, Irish, and Savoyards. Protestant Europe was outraged. Milton, as Cromwell's secretary, was called upon to write letters of protest to the duke, the Catholic king and cardinal of France, and other heads of state. His own indignant prayer to a God of wrath has, as William Riley Parker puts it, "the awesome sound of a great wave pounding against a wall."

Page 123. Christians at War. Text from the official "little red songbook" of the Wobblies, or the Industrial Workers of the World: *Songs of the Workers* (Chicago: I.W.W., edition of 1956).

Page 128. The Daughters of the Horseleech. Kunitz's poem refers to a great passage of biblical invective: the words of Agur, against a vile generation:

> There is a generation that curseth their father, and does not bless their mother. There is a generation that are pure in their own eyes, and yet is not washed from their filthiness. . . . There is a generation whose teeth are as swords, and their jaw teeth as knives, to devour the poor from off the earth, and the needy from among men. The horseleech hath two daughters, crying, Give, give. There are three things that are never satisfied, yea, four things say not, It is enough: The grave; and the barren womb; the earth that is not filled with water; and the fire that saith not, It is enough. The eye that mocketh at his father, and despiseth to obey his mother, the ravens of the valley shall pick it out, and the young eagles shall eat it. (Proverbs 30: 11–17)

Page 136. England in 1819 and **Similes for Two Political Characters of 1819.** During a rally in favor of parliamentary reforms in Manchester on August 19, 1819, troops attacked a crowd, causing the deaths of several citizens. Shelley was provoked to write a handful of angry political poems: besides these, the "Lines Written during the Castlereagh Administration," "The Mask of Anarchy," and the well-known "Song to the Men of England." In the Harvard manuscript, "Similes" is headed *To S———th and C———gh*: Home Secretary Sidmouth and Foreign Secretary Castlereagh. At the time, Castlereagh was also leader of Commons.

Page 139. On Lord Holland's Seat near Margate, Kent. First printed without Gray's consent in the *New Foundling Hospital for Wit*, 1769. Henry Fox, subject of the poem, who had lined his pockets comfortably as paymaster-general, had capped his career with elevation to the peerage. His venal friends, named in lines 17–18, had quarreled with Fox—now Baron Holland of Foxley—or had quit him for friends more influential. (For details, see Roger Lonsdale's annotated edition of *The Poems of Gray, Collins, and Goldsmith*, New

York: Norton, 1972, p. 263.) Holland's seat apparently displayed that fondness for artificial Roman wreckage to which free-spending eighteenth-century gentlemen were susceptible. Cowper, who in 1763 viewed the estate under construction, called it "a fine piece of ruins, built . . . at a great expense, which, the day after I saw it, tumbled down for nothing." Horace Walpole found the place "half-civilized"—hence, engaging. Around an allegedly correct replica of Cicero's villa at Baiae, Holland caused to be scattered (in Walpole's description) "buildings of all sorts, but in no style of architecture that ever appeared before or has since, and with no connection with or to one another, and in all directions."

Page 144. 'Last came, and last did go.' In the commonplace book he kept in Horton, Milton admired how Dante, in his Canto VII, deals with the avarice of the clergy. William Riley Parker has praised the "flesh-crawling harshness" of the line "Grate on their scrannel pipes of wretched straw," and recalls John Aubrey's observation that Milton, when satirical, "pronounced the letter *R* very hard" (*Milton: A Biography*, Oxford: Oxford University Press, 1968, p. 162). Scholars also have chewed long upon "that two-handed engine at the door." It is probably the same avenging two-handed sword that Michael wields in *Paradise Lost*, which blazes but does not strike as the archangel, with empty hands, kindly leads Adam and Eve out of Eden (XII, 633–40). Compare the punishing sword of God's word in Revelation 19: 13–15 and Hebrews 4: 12. Perhaps Milton sees it as a lightning bolt, as does his favorite poet, Spenser, to whom Jove's wrath is a "three-forked engine" (*Faerie Queene*, VII, 9). And why does it "smite once, and smite no more"? Because, as in the proverb, lightning never strikes twice in the same place.

Page 145. Holy Willie's Prayer. Although Burns did not print this satiric blast during his lifetime, copies of it were circulated, with the effect that (as the poet wrote to Dr. John Moore) it sufficiently "alarmed the kirk-Session that they held three several meetings to look over their holy artillery, if any of it was pointed against profane rhymers." Holy Willie, who smugly misunderstands Calvin's doctrine of election, was in life one William Fisher. Burns supplied background to the poem in the "Argument" he wrote for it: "Holy Willie was a rather oldish bachelor elder in the parish of Mauchline, and much and justly famed for that polemical chattering which ends in tippling orthodoxy, and for that spiritualized bawdry which refines to liquorish devotion. In a sessional process with a gentleman in Mauchline—a Mr. Gavin Hamilton— Holy Willie and his priest, Father Auld, after a full hearing in the Presbytery of Ayr, came off but second best, owing partly to the oratorical powers of Mr. Robert Aiken, Mr. Hamilton's counsel, but chiefly to Mr. Hamilton's being one of the most irreproachable and truly respectable characters in the county. On losing his process, the Muse overheard him at his devotions."

Page 149. Bagman O'Reilly's Curse. Writing from Chatswood, New South Wales, Les A. Murray supplied, along with permission to include this poem, a few specimens of verse from the distinguished Australian popular tradition of scurrility and vituperation. The most remarkable is "The Bastard from the Bush," a ballad known in part, according to Mr. Murray, "to most male Australians above the age of fourteen"; and apparently an ancestor in the line of invective leading to "Bagman O'Reilly's Curse." The folk ballad is about a superhero from the wilds who joins a "push," a gang of thugs who terrorized the slums of Sydney from the 1880s through the 1920s. When the gang, jealous of his prowess, turns against him, the Bastard singlehandedly thrashes the lot of them, inspiring this curse:

> "You low polluted bastard!"
> Snarled the captain of the push,
> "Get back to where your sort belong,
> That's somewhere in the bush!
> And may the following misfortunes
> Soon tumble down on you:
> May some poxy harlot dose you
> Till your bollocks turn sky-blue!
>
> "May the pains of windy spasms
> Through your worm-gnawed bowels dart;
> May you shit your bloody trousers
> Every time you try to fart;
> May you take a swig of pig's piss,
> Mistaking it for beer,
> May the next push you impose on
> Chuck you out upon your ear!
>
> "May the itching piles torment you;
> May corns grow on your feet;
> May crabs as big as spiders
> Attack your balls a treat;
> Then when you're down-and-outed
> To a hopeless bloody wreck,
> May you slip back through your arsehole
> And break your fucking neck!"

The ballad is attributed to Henry Lawson, and Mr. Murray's copy was typed out by a friend living in a place called Putty, in the bush about eighty miles north of Sydney. Bill Wannan gives a more literary version in his *Robust, Ribald, and Rude Verse in Australia* (Melbourne: Lansdowne Press, 1972).

Page 151. To Pius IX. "The writer of these lines," Whittier assured his readers, "is no enemy of Catholics." The pope had fled Rome in 1848, when revolutionists proclaimed the city a republic, and had been restored in 1850 with the aid of the French army.

Page 166. On the Author of a Play Called *Sodom.* Anthony à Wood, in his sketch of the life of Rochester, remarks that most anonymous obscene verse of the Restoration was "fathered upon the Earl . . . after he had obtained the name of an excellent smooth, but withall a most lewd poet." Apparently this was the case with *Sodom, or the Quintessence of Debauchery*, a five-act farce in heroic couplets. (Mild sample: *"Bolloxinion:* In ropy seed my spirit shall be sent / With joyful tidings to his fundament.") R. M. Baine has blamed the play upon Christopher Fishbourne.

Page 172. To Edward FitzGerald. Paging one Sunday through W. Aldis Wright's edition of *The Life and Letters of Edward FitzGerald*, Browning, then in his seventy-eighth year, discovered these sexist remarks in a FitzGerald letter of 1861:

> Mrs. Browning's death is rather a relief to me, I must say: no more Aurora Leighs, thank God! A woman of real Genius, I know; but what is the upshot of it all? She and her Sex had better mind the kitchen and their children; and perhaps the poor. Except in such things as little novels, they only devote themselves to what men do much better, leaving that which men do worse or not at all.

The next day Browning composed his retort to the dead FitzGerald, whom he had never met, and fired it off to the *Athenaeum*. The magazine's editor rushed it into type for his number of that Saturday, July 13, 1889, and ignored a telegram Browning sent him later in the week, seeking to retract it.

Page 174. Dulce et Decorum Est. In manuscript versions, this poem carries the dedication "To Jessie Pope" (a writer of patriotic verse apparently urging bigger and better bloodshed) or "To a certain Poetess."

Page 177. Valentine. Under the caustic title "Simple Annals of the Callous," Lee Wilson Dodd had roasted Hemingway's *Men Without Women* in the *Saturday Review of Literature* for November 19, 1927. Hemingway lists—in his poem's parenthesis—a few criticisms that Dodd and others had leveled at his work and at his gallusless hero, Jake Barnes. This valentine appeared in May 1929 in the last number of the *Little Review*, whose editor, Margaret Anderson, had invited contributions that "should not be literature." I am indebted for this information to a note by Nicholas Gerogiannis in his edition of Hemingway's *88 Poems* (New York: Harcourt Brace Jovanovich and Bruccoli Clark, 1979).

Page 179. On Philosophers. Sometimes attributed to Ben Jonson.

Page 183. Lines on Being Refused a Guggenheim Fellowship. Gordon N. Ray, president of the Guggenheim Foundation, writing in the foundation's annual report in 1979, remarked with some thankfulness that over the years few unsuccessful applicants had protested the foundation's decisions, but cited this public rebuke by John Hollander (from *Jiggery Pokery, A Compendium of Double Dactyls*, edited by Anthony Hecht and Hollander, New York: Atheneum, 1966):

NO FOUNDATION

Higgledy-piggledy
John Simon Guggenheim,
Honored wherever the
Muses collect,

Save in the studies (like
Mine) which have suffered his
Unjustifiable,
Shocking neglect.

Whittemore later received a Guggenheim grant to finish a biography of William Carlos Williams.

Page 196. Sam Hall. This desperate character, in some accounts, began life as a poor waif forced to sweep chimneys. A song about him became current in the 1790s; it derived from an earlier ballad of "Captain Kidd," and later evolved into "The Hanging Song," heard in music halls in Victorian days. See Bertrand H. Bronson, "Samuel Hall's Family Tree," *California Folklore Quarterly* 1 (1942): 47–64, and G. Legman's discussion in *The Horn Book* (New York: University Books, 1964), pp. 197, 382–83. About 1930, John A. Lomax heard this American version belted out by members of the Adventure Campfire Club at the University of California, Berkeley.

Page 199. The Hustler. This outrageous boast is a *toast*: a kind of poem recited by urban blacks involved in the sporting life. The speaker in "The Hustler" is a con man and a pimp, as Dennis Wepman, Ronald B. Newman, and Murray B. Binderman note in their monumental collection of toasts, *The Life: The Lore and Folk Poetry of the Black Hustler* (Philadelphia: University of Pennsylvania Press, 1976). They date the poem from shortly after the Clay-Liston fight in 1964. "Boxcar," an inmate of Auburn prison who supplied this text, said it came from Jersey City.

Page 205. Canto XLV. Not only splendid artists of the Renaissance are hailed in Pound's blast against commercialism, but also worthy patrons. Duke Gonzaga commissioned Mantegna to paint his family in fresco in the ducal palace in Mantua, about 1465. St. Trophime, in Arles, is renowned for its cloisters, set with double columns; St. Hilaire, in Poitiers, for (according to Pound) its proportion. Cramoisi is fine crimson cloth, woven in Greece. Hans Memling, fifteenth-century Flemish painter, decorated the reliquary shrine of St. Ursula in Bruges. Pound thought the Eleusinian mysteries an ideal community of mystics: "Eleusis did not distort truth by exaggerating the individual, neither could it have violated the individual spirit" (*Guide to Kulchur*, Norfolk, Conn.: New Directions, 1952, p. 299). Usury, in Pound's imagination, corrupts even the Eleusinian mysteries by substituting prostitution for ritual coition.

Page 206. [Envy]. Hateful portraits of the Seven Deadly Sins brightly burn in English poetry from the fourteenth through the sixteenth century. Besides Spenser's display of them, from which we take "Envy," other memorable characterizations of the Sins include Langland's in *Piers Plowman* (Passus V) and Marlowe's in *The Tragical History of Doctor Faustus* (II, ii).

Page 208. [Urizen's curse upon his children]. Two consecutive passages from *The Four Zoas*, Night the Sixth, are given here: Blake's manuscript pages 68 (lines 5–27) and 70 (lines 5–45). I have left out a long interjection by Tharmas; it interrupts the curse. Urizen's diatribe against his daughters might seem more naturally to belong among this book's poems of family strife; and indeed, perhaps it owes something to Lear's curse on Goneril. Blake's characters, however, are personified abstractions. Primarily, Urizen is human reason, which the poet distrusts—especially when it gets up on its high horse and renounces the flesh, passions, and human nature. Those elements of man are probably what Urizen's three daughters signify, although they cannot be labeled conveniently.

Page 225. Ancient Music. Despite a vow to resist parodies, I had to include Pound's famous take-off on the thirteenth-century English lyric that begins, "Sumer is icumen in, / Lhude sing cuccu! / Groweth sed and bloweth med / and springth the wode nu. / Sing cuccu!" (Harley manuscript 978, monks' commonplace-book from Reading Abbey). K. K. Ruthven has pointed out that, perhaps by coincidence, Frank Sidgwick was inspired to a parody of the same lyric in 1915, the year Pound first printed his own version. Sidgwick's opens: "Wynter ys icumen in, / Lhoudly syng *tish-ù*!" See also Paul Zimmer's "Zumer Is Icumen In" ("Lewdly sing whohoo") in *The Zimmer Poems* (Washington D.C. and San Francisco: Dryad, 1976).

Page 241. [Lines written during a period of insanity]. This skilled finger-exercise in classical measures seems to have been composed in or about 1774, and first appeared in Cowper's posthumous *Memoirs* (London, 1816). As H. S. Milford notes in his edition of Cowper's *Poetical Works*, the poem is strikingly similar to Francis Davison's earlier "Sapphics, Upon the Passion of Christ," which begins, "Hatred Eternal, furious revenging." Cowper deserves to shine among the major English poets of invective, and is to be credited also with the powerful ironic attack on slave-trading, "Sweet Meat Has Sour Sauce"; with "Olney Hymn" LVII ("Hatred of sin"); and with epigrams such as this, written in 1780:

> False, cruel, disappointed, stung to th'heart,
> France quits the warrior's for th'assassin's part;
> To dirty hands a dirty bribe conveys,
> Bids the low street and lofty palace blaze.
> Her sons too weak to vanquish us alone,
> She hires the worst and basest of her own.—
> Kneel, France!—a suppliant conquers us with ease,
> We always spare a coward on his knees.

Page 251. Introducing a Madman. Apparently a "found poem," this is, according to its author, "an abridgment of Bram Stoker's *Dracula*."

Page 258. I Hate That Drum's Discordant Sound. Also known as John Scott of Amwell, this Quaker poet was the author of *Observations on the State of the Parochial and Vagrant Poor* (1773).

INDEX OF POETS

Quotations that appear in the Introduction, on part-title pages, and in the notes are indicated by page numbers in italics.